Grade 3

Oh, Yeah? ✓ Proof It!

Frank Schaffer
An imprint of Carson-Dellosa Publishing LLC
Greensboro, North Carolina

Frank Schaffer Publications®
An imprint of Carson-Dellosa Publishing LLC
P.O. Box 35665
Greensboro, NC 27425 USA

© 2010 Carson-Dellosa Publishing LLC. The purchase of this material entitles the buyer to reproduce worksheets and activities for classroom use only—not for commercial resale. Reproduction of these materials for an entire school or district is prohibited. No part of this book may be reproduced (except as noted above), stored in a retrieval system, or transmitted in any form or by any means (mechanically, electronically, recording, etc.) without the prior written consent of Carson-Dellosa Publishing LLC. Frank Schaffer is an imprint of Carson-Dellosa Publishing LLC.

Printed in the USA • All rights reserved.   ISBN 0-7682-3653-3

1 2 3 4 5 6 7 8 9 10 GLO 15 14 13 12 11 10

TABLE OF CONTENTS

Letter from the Publisher

Teachers, Family Members, and Other Caregivers:

Proofreading is an essential skill when writing and evaluating the writing of others. As students grow more skilled in proofreading, they hone their ability to quickly spot and correct their own errors, as well as the errors of classmates. This heightens their awareness of grammar and other skills necessary to write well.

Oh, Yeah? Proof It! is designed with a scaffolded approach. Proofreading skills are initially isolated. Then, they are integrated into the writing tasks with skills already addressed. Ultimately, students are called upon to exercise all the proofreading skills they have learned throughout the book. Such scaffolding allows students to experience a mastery and confidence with specific skills before moving ahead to tackle others. This approach ultimately prepares them for the wrap-up activities that appear at the end of the book, as well as proofreading they will engage in throughout their lives.

Sincerely,
Frank Schaffer Publications

PROOFREADING MARKS

This is how you show a change from a capital letter to a lowercase letter.

Ɖoctor

This is how you show a change from a lowercase letter to a capital letter.

chicago

Use this mark to add a period if it is missing.

Tues.

Use this mark to add an end mark.

This is my dog.

Is this my dog?

What a dog!

This is how you take out an end mark and add a new end mark.

Is this my dog. ?

Use this mark to add a comma.

Houston, Texas

Use this mark to add a quotation mark.

Don said, "Let's go home."

This is how you move a quotation mark to a new location.

"Don said, "Let's go home."

Use this mark to add underlining.

Ramona Quimby, Age 8

Use this mark to take away underlining.

Ramona Quimby, Age 8

Use this mark to add an apostrophe.

dont

Use this mark to take away an apostrophe.

don't

Use this mark to take away a word or a letter.

I don't not like

Nobody never goes there.

This is how to take away one word or letter and add another.

their
They left there bats in the gym.

Use this mark to show a new paragraph.

¶

NEWS

Read the article. The writer has made some mistakes with capital letters. Use marks to correct the mistakes.

Four Corners

by Rick Sanchez

Anika Ross has stood in four States at the same time! Anika is one of the new Students in third Grade this year. she is in Mr. dald's class. Anika moved to our Town from new mexico.

Anika has shared many interesting Stories about her life in new mexico. there are excellent hiking trails near her old home. her family often went on Hikes.

Anika enjoys Soccer. she was the star Goalie on her old team. Anika is looking forward to the tryouts for our School's team.

what was Anika's most interesting story of all? She has stood in four States at one time. Really! Did you know that i can do this? others can do

---

CAPITAL LETTERS

- Every sentence must begin with a capital letter.
  This is my book.

- A common noun does not begin with a capital letter and names a person, place, or thing. It does not name a specific person, place, or thing.
  Common Nouns: dog, city, doctor

- A proper noun begins with a capital letter and names a specific person, place, or thing.
  Proper Nouns: Rover, Chicago, Doctor Gomez

- The word *I* is always capitalized.
  She and I went to the store.

- This is how you show a change from a capital letter to a lowercase letter.
  Ɖoctor

- This is how you show a change from a lowercase letter to a capital letter.
  chicago

---

this, too. How? they can visit the four corners monument.

where is the four corners monument? and how can People stand in four States at once there? Take a look at a map. you will see that arizona, colorado, utah, and new mexico all share a boundary. This boundary is at the four corners monument. When you stand at the monument, this is the Place where all four States meet.

we welcome anika to our School. we all look forward to getting to know her better.

Now, write a news article of your own.

☐ Include an article title and your name.

☐ Tell details of an exciting or interesting event that happened in your town.

☐ Include the names of people for the story.

☐ Include the name of your town.

☐ Make sure to begin all sentences with a capital letter.

☐ Make sure to begin all common nouns with a lowercase letter.

☐ Make sure to begin all proper nouns with a capital letter.

_____

_____

_____

_____

_____

_____

_____

_____

_____

_____

_____

_____

TIGER NEWS

NEWS

Read the article. The writer has made some mistakes with capital letters. Use proofreading marks to correct the mistakes.

REMEMBER!
- Begin a sentence with a capital letter.
- Begin a proper noun with a capital letter.
- The word *I* is always capitalized.

Interview with Hassan Janara

by Claire Grand

This week, i interviewed Hassan Janara about his Cousin's Company. hassan's cousin takes People on Tours at the statue of liberty when they visit new york city. visitors must ride on a Boat to get to the Statue.

Hassan told me about his visit to the statue of liberty. His Cousin explained that the statue was planned and built in france. It was planned by a Sculptor named frederic auguste bartholdi.

The Statue was too big to ship to the united states. workers had to take it apart! Then, they packed the 350 pieces and put them on a ship.

People in the united states had to raise Money to pay for a base for the Statue. It took a great deal of work to put the Statue together and place it on the base.

hassan's Cousin told Visitors that the torch held in the statue's right Hand burned for a very long time. But the torch started to wear out, and it was damaged by Water. it was replaced by an electric torch.

hassan can't wait to visit his Cousin in new york city again. On his next Trip, He hopes to go to Art Museums and tour a Television Station.

GO!

Note the changes you made to the article. Then, rewrite the article correctly.

_____

_____

_____

_____

_____

_____

_____

_____

_____

_____

_____

_____

_____

_____

_____

_____

CLASSIFIEDS

Read the ad. The writer has made some mistakes with capital letters. Use proofreading marks to correct the mistakes.

REMEMBER!

- Begin a sentence with a capital letter.
- Begin a proper noun with a capital letter. Don't forget that days of the week, months of the year, and holidays begin with a capital letter.
- The word *I* is always capitalized.
- Remember what you learned about the marks for capital and lowercase letters.

Ɗoctor

chicago

Bike World Sale

Come to Bike World! We have the finest bikes in miami.

The first five People who come on monday, march 5, will receive free bike Horns.

---

bike world

691 ling street

miami, Florida

---

we have the best prices in our City!

The sale will last all Week.

The sale will start on monday, march 5.

The sale will end on sunday, march 11.

do not miss this great sale!

Ask shop owner maria sanchez about special prices for Students from zane elementary school.

don't forget to check back for our big sale on july 4, independence day.

Correctly rewrite the ad.

Bike World Sale

BOOK REVIEW

Read the book review. The writer has made some mistakes with capital letters in titles of poems, songs, and books. Use proofreading marks to correct the mistakes.

REMEMBER!

- Use a capital letter to begin the first word in a song, poem, book, or play title.
- Use a capital letter to begin important words in a song, poem, book, or play title.
- In a title, do not use a capital letter to begin the unimportant words *a, an, the, in,* or *of* unless the word is the first word of the title.

The Wizard of Oz

Cam Jansen and the
Mystery of the Dinosaur Bones

Sarah, plain And Tall

by Miyoko Chong

I was excited about writing this book review. The book was excellent. The characters' adventures made me think about the song with the title "we are On The trail." Why? The characters live on the prairie. They give the reader a feeling of being on a trail and going in a direction to find home.

The main characters at the beginning of the book are a father and his children, Caleb and Anna. The father writes to Sarah. She is in Maine. She comes to visit the family. Everyone gets along well.

Still, Sarah misses her old home far away. The father and his children don't want Sarah to leave. Does she stay, or does she go? Guess you'll have to read the book to discover the answer.

I was inspired by this book written by Patricia MacLachlan. I was so inspired that I wrote a poem about living on the prairie. The title of the poem is "Living To Work And working To Live."

Next month, our school drama club will do a play based on the book. The play is called "a new Life For Caleb And Anna." I plan to write a review of the play next month. Watch for it in our newspaper.

A. *Correctly rewrite all of the titles from the article.*

_____

_____

_____

_____

B. *Correctly write titles below. Underline the book title. Place quotation marks around poem, play, and song titles.*

The title of one of my favorite books:

The title of one of my favorite songs:

The title of one of my favorite poems:

The title of one of my favorite plays:

Read the letter. The writer has made some mistakes with capital letters. Use proofreading marks to correct the mistakes.

REMEMBER!

- Use a capital letter for the first word in a song, poem, book, or play title.
- Use a capital letter to begin important words in a song, poem, book, or play title.
- In a title, do not use a capital letter to begin the unimportant words *a, an, the, in,* or *of* unless the word is the first word of the title.
- Begin a sentence with a capital letter.
- Begin a proper noun with a capital letter. Days of the week, months of the year, and holidays begin with a capital letter.
- The word *I* is always capitalized.

Lunchroom Changes

september 15, 2011

Dear Ms. tran:

We've seen big changes in the Lunchroom at king elementary school during the past few Years. there is one more change many of us would like to see. We would like to have healthy pizza choices. Last Week, i read "How To make A Healthy pizza." This magazine article had many good Ideas. It was written by someone who lives in california. in california, there have already been many healthy Changes in lunchroom Menus.

i have asked ten Students in each grade for ideas about menu items. everyone has offered pizza as a suggestion. We know the Cooks can use low-fat cheese and whole-wheat crust. We would also like to see Vegetables added as toppings.

maybe we could start the changes in october. If it's hard for the cooks to prepare the pizza, maybe we could just have pizza twice a Week. Maybe we could have Pizza on tuesdays and fridays. Thank you for your time. And thank you for thinking about making this Change.

Sincerely,

Rico Jones

rico jones

GO!

Correctly rewrite the letter.

CLASSIFIEDS

Read the ad. The writer has made some mistakes with capital letters. Use proofreading marks to correct the mistakes.

Let's Sell Wrapping Paper!

it's that time of the Year again! we will be selling wrapping paper to make money for carver elementary school. All the Teachers will have forms to give to their Students.

We hope to have huge sales for our School.

The sale will begin wednesday, october 10. It will continue until the Week after thanksgiving. Tell all your Friends and Neighbors. show them the samples.

Your teacher will tell you about parts of

the book titled <u>how To sell wrapping paper</u>.

this will give you good Ideas for selling.

Now, correctly rewrite the ad.

Let's Sell Wrapping Paper!

SCHEDULE

Read the schedule for activities after school. The writer has made some mistakes with abbreviations. Use proofreading marks to correct the abbreviation mistakes.

REMEMBER!

• An abbreviation is a short way to write a word. Almost all abbreviations begin with a capital letter and end with a period.

Mon.   Tues.   Aug.   Sept.

• Remember what you learned about the marks for capital and lowercase letters.

Doctor

tues.

Tues.

Schedule for Activities after School

This schedule shows Ms Johnson's music practices and mr Saldovar's art practices.

It is the schedule for mon through fri for next week.

Week of dec 10 through dec 16

mon	Tues	wed	thurs.	fri
piano	violin	saxophone	clarinet	cello
painting	sculpture	woodworking	drawing	sketching

GO!

First, write the schedule correctly.

_____

_____

_____

_____

_____

_____

_____

_____

_____

_____

_____

_____

_____

_____

Now, write your own schedule.

☐ Include the abbreviation for the month.

☐ Include activities for at least three days of the week.

☐ Use abbreviations for the days of the week.

_____

_____

_____

_____

_____

_____

_____

_____

_____

_____

_____

_____

Read the article. The writer has made some mistakes with abbreviations. Use marks to correct the mistakes.

New Teachers and Principal

by Jo Lene

We have new teachers and a new principal this year.

Please make them all feel welcome!

Here is the list.

Principal: dr Gonzales

Teachers

Kindergarten: mr Delfino

Grade 1: Ms Wong

Grade 2: ms. Shakim

Grade 4: Mr Saldovar

Grade 5: mr Jones and ms Parker

GO!

A. *Correctly rewrite the list of teachers.*

_____

_____

_____

_____

_____

_____

_____

B. *Write the names of your principal and five teachers you have now or have had in the past. Use abbreviations for their titles.*

_____

_____

_____

_____

_____

_____

_____

COMICS

Read the comic. Use proofreading marks to correct the mistakes with capital letters and abbreviations.

Gift Trick on Fri., Apr. 1

by April Foolish

wow, look at all the gifts from your Aunts and Uncles! Did you get your Mom's and your Grandpa's presents already, too?

Oh yeah, i got them. But i wasn't happy about them.

what do you mean? why weren't you happy?

every single gift was the same video game. The game has the same title as one of my favorite Books, Racing in time.

oh, i get it! your birthday is on april fool's day.

yes, every single year.

At least your family is creative Our teacher, ms Homish, says that creativity is a good thing.

maybe I'll just need to think of something creative on their Birthdays next Year!

Now, correctly rewrite the comic.

Gift Trick on Fri., Apr. 1

by April Foolish

LETTERS TO THE EDITOR

Read the letter to the editor. The writer has made some mistakes with end marks. Use proofreading marks to correct the mistakes.

REMEMBER!

- A statement ends with a period.
  This is my dog.

- A question ends with a question mark.
  Is this my dog?

- An exclamation ends with an exclamation mark.
  What a dog!

- A command usually ends with a period.
  Please close the door.

- Use this mark to take out an end mark.
  Is this my dog?

- Use this mark to add an end mark.
  This is my dog.
  Is this my dog?
  What a dog!

- This is how to replace one end mark with a different end mark.
  Is this my dog. ?

School Play

Dear Editor:

I read the letter to the editor last week The letter said we should not have the school play this year It said we should spend the money on sports instead. Why should we have to give up the school play. What a shame to lose this event?

Many of us would be happy to have a bake sale to raise more money for the play What else could we do. We could have a car wash or do another activity? How sad it would be to lose the play.

We hope we will be able to vote on this The students who are actors are willing to work hard to keep our school play?

Sincerely,

Tammy Cruz

Tammy Cruz

GO!

Correctly rewrite the letter.

_____

_____

_____

_____

_____

_____

_____

_____

_____

_____

_____

_____

_____

_____

_____

_____

_____

_____

_____

_____

CLASSIFIEDS

Read the ad. The writer has made some mistakes with capital letters, abbreviations, and end marks. Use proofreading marks to correct the mistakes.

REMEMBER!

Remember what you have learned about capital letters, abbreviations, and end marks. Turn to page 5 if you need to review the marks.

The Fair

The school fair is coming up soon at thomas jefferson elementary school?

It will be on sat., apr 10. What fun this will be for the whole family?

The Fair will start at 10:00 in the morning.

It will end at sunset?

We will have the Fair at the Park at 345 maple lane.

there will be games, prizes, and food You can buy Tickets

in the office from mon through Fri the week before the fair?

tell your friends and neighbors to come to the Fair. Everyone

in the Community is welcome. The Money from the Fair

will help us buy new Computers for the School.

Do you want to go to a planning meeting!

Go to Ms chapman's room after school on thurs afternoon.

Read the marks you have made. Correctly rewrite the ad.

The Fair

BLOG POST

Read the blog post. The writer has made some mistakes with commas. Use proofreading marks to correct the mistakes.

REMEMBER!

- Use a comma between the date and the year.

  May 30, 2012

- Use a comma between the name of a city and its state.

  Houston, Texas

- Use a comma after the opening in a letter, e-mail, or blog post to a friend.

  Dear Ling,

- Use a comma after the first line of the closing in a letter.

  Sincerely,
  Anita

- Use this mark to add a comma.

  Houston Texas

- Use this mark to take out a comma.

  May, 30, 2012

New Clubs

Dear Juan

I saw the letter to the editor about new clubs for the school. I think this is a very good idea. I read about an elementary school in Seattle Washington. Students there started a new club program on September, 5 2010. There were clubs for the interests of many students.

I would like to see new clubs here in our school before February 10 2012. I will be happy to talk to students to ask about the kinds of clubs they would like. Maybe you could print the list of new clubs we would like. Thank you.

Sincerely

Greg Lands

Oh, Yeah? Proof It! Grade 3

A. *Read the proofreading marks you have made. Correctly rewrite Greg's letter to the editor.*

_____

_____

_____

_____

_____

_____

_____

B. *Write your own short letter to the editor.*

☐ Write about a change you would like to have at your school.

☐ Include a greeting.

☐ Include the name of a city and its state.

☐ Include at least one date with the month, day, and year.

☐ Include a closing.

_____

_____

_____

_____

RECIPE

Read this article about a recipe. The writer has made some mistakes with commas. Use proofreading marks to correct the mistakes.

REMEMBER!

- Use a comma after these words when they begin a sentence: *well, yes, no, now, next, finally, today, yesterday, tomorrow, first, second, third,* and other words to tell time order.

  Yes, let's go.

- Use commas to separate words in a series. A series is a list of three or more words.

  We bought eggs, cheese, and bread.

- Remember what you learned about marks for commas.

- Use this mark to add a comma.

  Houston Texas

- Use this mark to take out a comma.

  May, 30, 2012

Burritos

by Jan Smart

Yesterday I spent the day with my grandpa. We made burritos for lunch. Would you like to make burritos? This is how to make them.

You will need beans cheese and lettuce. You will also need soft tacos.

First put a soft taco on a plate. Next add the beans cheese and lettuce. Finally roll up the soft taco. Well that's all you have to do to make this tasty treat!

Do you have a recipe or idea for a tasty treat? Send it to the newspaper. Share it with the school. The newspaper prints recipes from teachers students and their friends. We look forward to hearing from you!

Now, write an easy recipe of your own. You might write how to make fruit salad or how to make a sandwich.

☐ Include an article title and your name.

☐ Tell the name of the food in the title.

☐ Include a series of at least three items needed.

☐ Include at least one of these words: *first, next, finally.*

☐ Tell the steps to make the food.

_____

_____

_____

_____

_____

_____

_____

_____

_____

_____

_____

_____

_____

_____

PLAY REVIEW

Read the play review. The writer has made some mistakes with commas. Use marks to correct the mistakes.

"On the Farm"

by Julia Pober

REMEMBER!

- Use a comma after these words when they begin a sentence: *well, yes, no, now, next, finally, today, yesterday, tomorrow, first, second, third,* and other words to tell time order.

  Yes, let's go.

- Use commas to separate words in a series. A series is a list of three or more words.

  We bought eggs, cheese, and bread.

- Remember what you learned about marks for commas.

- Use this mark to add a comma.

  Houston, Texas

- Use this mark to take out a comma.

  May, 30, 2012

I am happy to review the school play. "On the Farm" was an excellent show. The actors included students from grades two three and four. Well I must say they all did a fine job.

There were a few problems with the show. First the curtain wouldn't open. Next part of the curtain fell on the stage. But the show did go on!

The beginning of the play showed farmers, neighbors, and friends working together. There had been very little rain. Yes the farmers were sad and worried. Everyone was trying to keep the crops alive.

Next the middle of the play showed that some of the crops were dying. Finally farmers had a big meeting with the community. Everyone talked thought and planned.

Did the farmers succeed? No I'm not going to tell you the answer. You should go see the play for yourself to find out. Support our drama club. Go see the play next weekend!

Correctly rewrite the play review.

_____

_____

_____

_____

_____

_____

_____

_____

_____

_____

_____

_____

_____

_____

_____

_____

_____

_____

TIGER NEWS
STUDENT STORIES

Read the story. The writer has made some mistakes with commas. Use proofreading marks to correct the mistakes.

REMEMBER!

• Use a comma after a person's name at the beginning of a sentence.

"Al, I have your book."

• Use a comma before the beginning quotation mark in dialogue—words that are spoken.

She said, "Here is your present."

I asked, "What is it?"

• Use this mark to add a comma.

Houston‸Texas

"Watching the Sailboats"

by Nav Facs

Ellie and Jamil went to the lake with their dad. The water sparkled. Birds flew. Sailboats dotted the water. Jamil said "This is the most beautiful day ever!"

Their dad said "Lunchtime!" Ellie and Jamil dashed to the picnic table.

Dad asked "Ellie what would you like on your hot dog?"

Ellie said "Dad you know I like my hot dog plain."

Dad asked Jamil what he wanted on his hot dog.

Jamil answered "Dad don't be silly. I like everything on my hot dog!"

After lunch, Ellie and Jamil played in the lake. Then they heard a rumble of thunder.

Dad shouted "It's time to get out of the water."

The three raced to the car. Ellie said, "Jamil this might have been the most beautiful day ever. But it didn't last!"

Everyone laughed. Dad said "Ellie we'll come back to the lake next month."

Now, correctly rewrite the story.

FROM THE BLOG

Read the blog. The writer has made some mistakes with commas. Use proofreading marks to correct the mistakes.

REMEMBER!

- Use a comma after these words when they begin a sentence: *well, yes, no, now, next, finally, today, yesterday, tomorrow, first, second, third,* and other words to tell time order.

  Yes, let's go.

- Use commas to separate words in a series. A series is a list of three or more words.

  We bought eggs, cheese, and bread.

- Use a comma after a person's name at the beginning of a sentence.

  "Al, I have your book."

- Use a comma before the beginning quotation mark in dialogue. Dialogue is words on the page that are spoken.

  She said, "Here is your present."

  I asked, "What is it?"

- Use this mark to add a comma.

  Houston⌄Texas

Lost Dog!

Esparanza has lost her dog. She has written this newspaper blog post to ask everyone to help her find it. She says "Friends please help me find my dog. He means so much to my family." Esparanza has written this post to tell more about her lost dog.

Dear Students and Teachers:

Please help me find my dog. He ran away yesterday. His name is Coco. He is still a puppy. He was born on May 19 2011. Coco is brown black and red. Yesterday Ms. Shankar saw Coco near school. But she could not catch him. My neighbors have seen Coco near the park the library and our house. We are all trying very hard to find him. Please call me right away if you see him. Thank you!

Sincerely

Esparanza Juarez

GO!

Now, correctly rewrite blog.

_____

_____

_____

_____

_____

_____

_____

_____

_____

_____

_____

_____

_____

_____

_____

_____

_____

_____

_____

_____

LETTERS TO THE EDITOR

Read the letter. The writer has made some mistakes with capital letters, abbreviations, end marks, and commas. Use proofreading marks to correct the mistakes.

REMEMBER!

Remember what you have learned about capital letters, abbreviations, end marks, and commas. Turn to page 5 if you need to review the marks.

Tasty Delights

Dear Mr Ruma:

I was interested to read the tuesday interview with Dena Leighton. And i was surprised that her Company produces ice cream milk and cheese. In the interview, she said "My family has been in this Business for 100 years."

It was also interesting that her family started the Company the day after thanksgiving. That time of Year is often a time for People to relax But Ms leighton's family was working hard? What a family?

I would like to read Ms Leighton's book The article said the title is <u>my life In An ice cream factory</u>. That is the perfect name for the Book. I hope the book tells about the time her Aunt said "Dena ice cream is now your life."

Thank You for printing the interview. I enjoyed reading it.

Sincerely

Olga Pimmer

Olga Pimmer

GO!

Now, correctly rewrite the letter.

_____

_____

_____

_____

_____

_____

_____

_____

_____

_____

_____

_____

_____

_____

_____

_____

_____

_____

TIGER NEWS

NEWS

Read the article. The writer has made some mistakes with quotation marks. Use proofreading marks to correct the mistakes.

REMEMBER!

- Use quotation marks to show exactly the words someone says. These can be words said by a character in a story. The words can also be said by someone in real life. Usually, the end mark goes inside the quotation marks.

    Don said, "Let's go home."

    Chitra asked, "What time is it?"

- Use this mark to add a quotation mark.

    Don said, "Let's go home."

Successful School Bake Sale

by Hua Chong

The bake sale was a huge success. Mr. Delfy said, We made $3,000.00 for the school." He explained that students from all grades had worked hard to plan the sale.

Aisha Moore is in third grade. She said, "I was glad to have a chance to help plan such an important event.

Aisha's entire family pitched in to bake and sell. Her dad asked, When will we start planning for next year?"

Mr. Delfy answered, "We'll start planning in the fall next year. We would really appreciate your help again.

Glen Davis is in fourth grade. He said, I will definitely be a part of the bake sale again next year. Glen was in charge of cookies.

Ms. Win took a break from coaching to take charge of one of the tables at the bake sale. She exclaimed, "This is like having a new kind of teamwork!

Students and their families will be invited to help next year, too.

GO!

Now, write a news article or imaginary story of your own.

☐ Include an article title and your name.

☐ Write about something that has happened in your school or town. You may write about something real, or you may write a story that is not real.

☐ Include the exact words spoken by at least three people.

_____

_____

_____

_____

_____

_____

_____

_____

_____

_____

_____

_____

_____

_____

_____

CLASSIFIEDS

Read the ad. The writer has made some mistakes with quotation marks and underlining. Use proofreading marks to correct the mistakes.

REMEMBER!

- Use quotation marks for the title of a song.
  "The Star-Spangled Banner"

- Use quotation marks for the title of a short story or play.
  "Going to Town"

- Underline the title of a book.
  Ramona Quimby, Age 8

- Remember the proofreading mark to add a quotation mark.
  Don said, "Let's go home."

- Use this mark to add underlining.
  Ramona Quimby, Age 8

Between the Pages

Between the Pages is the best bookstore in town!

We have everything you're looking for. See our specials below.

Books on Sale

Henry and the Paper Route

The Best School Year Ever

Charlotte's Web

Sheet Music is on sale for these songs. We have songs for all ages.

Twinkle, Twinkle, Little Star

All You Need is Love

The Wheels on the Bus

We have all of these plays!

Traveling on the Road

Ayn and Rand

The Great Review

We have books filled with short stories like these.

Aladdin and the Wonderful Lamp

Three Words of Wisdom

Grand Adventures

Now, write one title in each box below.

☐ *Use titles for stories, books, and plays you have read.*

☐ *Use the title of a song you have heard.*

☐ *Be sure to use the correct punctuation for each title.*

☐ *Do not write the same titles you read in the ad.*

Book

_____

_____

_____

Song

_____

_____

_____

Play

_____

_____

_____

Short Story

_____

_____

_____

STUDENT STORIES

Read the letter. The writer has made some mistakes with capital letters, abbreviations, end marks, commas, quotation marks, and other punctuation. Use proofreading marks to correct the mistakes.

REMEMBER!

• Remember what you have learned about capital letters, abbreviations, and end marks. Remember what you have learned about commas, quotation marks, and other punctuation.

• Remember marks for capital letters. Remember marks for adding or taking away. Turn to page 5 if you need to review the marks.

Greetings from Earth

by Nita Hamlin

This week's story is science fiction It is written in the form of a letter to creatures on another Planet? The letter is from a visitor to Earth.

Dear Grillo

I am writing to tell you about something very strange I was visiting another Planet? I arrived on monday july 4 There were odd things happening all around Me.

First I saw creatures carrying heavy things with pages. One human said I'm glad we checked out this book from the Library." These words were on the front of the book: How To Celebrate independence Day.

Next i heard loud noises. A human asked a friend "Did you tell mr franklin to meet us for the fireworks. I wasn't sure what fireworks were. Finally I saw bright colors in the sky The humans seemed very happy? This must be a custom on their Planet.

i will be glad to get back to our Planet. it will be nice for things to be normal again.

Sincerely

Griblit

Griblit

GO!

Now, correctly rewrite the information before the letter. Then, correctly rewrite the letter.

STUDENT POETRY CORNER

Read the poem. The writer has forgotten some apostrophes. Use proofreading marks to add the apostrophes.

REMEMBER!

- Two words can be put together and made shorter to form a contraction.

  do + not = don't

  can + not = can't

  I + am = I'm

  you + would = you'd

- Use this mark to add an apostrophe.

  dont

- Use this mark to take away an apostrophe.

  don't

Dream On!

by Reve Craddock

I think Im trapped.

I cant get out.

My throat is tight,

but I wont shout.

Im' pounding the door

and kicking the wood.

It doesnt open

as it should.

Ill try to yell.

Ill try to scream.

I ha'dnt planned

on this bad dream.

I see a friend.

Ill look ahead.

Well hope this dream

w'ont cause more dread.

And then the light

comes into sight.

Ill open up my eyes.

Now Im awake

Its time to take

a step into the day.

No. Wait!

Id rather sleep longer instead.

Read your proofreading marks. Then, correctly rewrite the poem.

_____

_____

_____

_____

_____

_____

_____

_____

_____

_____

_____

_____

_____

_____

_____

_____

TIGER NEWS
SPORTS PAGE

Read the sports report. The writer has made some mistakes with apostrophes. Use proofreading marks to correct the mistakes.

REMEMBER!

- Use a possessive noun to show that someone owns something. For most singular nouns, add an apostrophe and the letter *s*.

    girl's hat

    friend's skates

    dog's tail

- For most plural nouns, add an apostrophe after the *s*.

    two girls' hats

    three friends' skates

    four dogs' tails

- Use this mark to add an apostrophe.

    girls

Our Team Wins!

by Pat Stroger

We have the best basketball team in the city! Our teams players were amazing in the game last week. Each players hard work was clear.

Students filled the gym before the game began. Many students shirts showed the teams name.

Play was tough during the beginning of the game. All the parents voices were hushed. Everyone watched.

The coaches voices were loud as they called out to players. We all watched and listened. The gym was very quiet before a big play. Then, one boys drink spilled onto the gym floor. Everyone had to wait for the floor to be cleaned. Finally, the game started again.

We weren't sure until the end who would win. At the last minute, we won! The players cheers were very loud. We are now the city champions!

Oh, Yeah? Proof It! Grade 3

GO!

Now, correctly rewrite the sports report.

_____

_____

_____

_____

_____

_____

_____

_____

_____

_____

_____

_____

_____

_____

_____

_____

_____

_____

_____

_____

TIGER NEWS
NEWS

Read the article. The writer has made some mistakes with apostrophes. Use proofreading marks to correct the mistakes.

Tornado Hits Our Town

by Shane Ville

A tornado hit our town last week. It hit at night. Most of us werent' outside. We were at home asleep. Many of us didnt even hear the tornado or the warning siren. No one in town was hurt.

Our schools front door was blown open. Water, paper, and leaves were blown into the main hall. Workers came to help the next morning. At first, they couldnt even see the floor underneath everything that had blown inside the hall. Then they cleared away the mess.

The teacher's said theyd like to return to school as soon as possible. But one teachers room was still a mess on Wednesday. Other teachers rooms did not take too long to clean. School should be open again next week. Well have to make up the lost days at the beginning of summer vacation.

Id like to thank the teachers who helped us put together this issue of the newspaper. I cant' imagine it would have been possible without them.

GO!

Now, correctly rewrite the news article.

_____

_____

_____

_____

_____

_____

_____

_____

_____

_____

_____

_____

_____

_____

_____

_____

_____

STUDENT POETRY CORNER

Read the poem. The writer has made some mistakes with capital letters, abbreviations, commas, quotation marks, and apostrophes. Use proofreading marks to correct the mistakes.

REMEMBER!

Remember what you have learned about capital letters, abbreviations, and end marks. Remember what you have learned about commas, quotation marks, and other punctuation. Turn to page 5 if you need to review the marks.

Birthday surprises

by Linus Paolo

I checked the Mail.

It was there!

I quickly ripped it open

I saw a card a note and a bit of cash.

This was exactly what Id been hoping.

The Birthday money was what Id wanted.

I took the card inside

I called my Aunt.

I said, "Im so happy that i could almost cry.

My Aunt was happy that I was glad

She told Me right away.

And then she had another surprise

She said I'm coming to see you next tuesday.

my birthday surprises were nearly complete.

What a wonderful day?

I couldn't wait to see my Aunt.

We could go together to Ms Rob's store to spend

my cash—right on my Birthday!

GO!

Now, correctly rewrite the poem.

_____

_____

_____

_____

_____

_____

_____

_____

_____

_____

_____

_____

_____

_____

_____

_____

BOOK REVIEW

Read the book review. The writer has made some errors with negative words. Use proofreading marks to correct the mistakes.

REMEMBER!

- A negative word is a word that has a meaning like *no* or *not*.

- Read these negative words.
  no not nothing never nowhere nobody

- Do not use two negative words together. This includes negative contractions. Here are some examples.
  didn't couldn't wouldn't can't won't
  doesn't hadn't shouldn't

- Use this mark to take away a word.

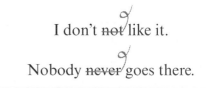

I don't ~~not~~ like it.

Nobody ~~never~~ goes there.

Planets

by Gita Chitra

This book isn't not the kind of book we usually review. We haven't never written this kind of review before now. Last week, the second graders wrote books about the stars and planets. We are reviewing one of the student's books.

This book does a good job of telling about the solar system. There's not nothing more interesting than a good book. And this book is very good.

The book gives information about Pluto. The writer explains that Pluto is not nowhere near Earth. The book says that Pluto is no longer named as a planet. No one never thought this would happen.

I think this student might grow up to be a writer. Her book is very interesting.

GO!

Now, correctly rewrite the book review.

_____

_____

_____

_____

_____

_____

_____

_____

_____

_____

_____

_____

_____

_____

_____

_____

_____

_____

_____

_____

CLASSIFIEDS

Read the ad. The writer has confused some words. Correct the writer's mistakes.

REMEMBER!

- There are some words that often confuse writers and readers. It is important to remember the correct spelling for each meaning of these words.

  their they're there

  to too two

  were we're where

  your you're

  here hear

  its it's

  who's whose

- Use these marks to take away one word and add another.

  their of
  They left ~~there~~ bats in the gym.

Help after the Hurricane

People in Louisiana need everyone's help after the big hurricane. The school is placing this add to let you no how everyone hear can help. We will be collecting items all weak.

Please take time to read all the information in this add. Were all sure you can find a weigh to help. If you have questions after you have red the add, call the school office.

We will bee collecting bottled water in the mall parking lot. This is the address.

425 Old River Rode

Take tops, slacks, and other close too the gym at the high school. Its at the back of the building.

We will knot turn away any help you want to offer, sew please call if you have more ideas.

Now, correctly rewrite the ad.

Help after the Hurricane

_____

_____

_____

_____

_____

_____

Read the article. The writer has confused some words. Use proofreading marks to take away the incorrect words and add the correct words.

Get to Know Our Class Leaders: Class President

by John Presley

Our class president is Lola Fein. I interviewed her last week. Lola moved hear from Michigan. She goes back their to visit her grandparents to times every year. They're cabin is near the lake, so Lola especially enjoys summer visits their. Her sister goes on the trips, to.

I talked to Lola about her ideas for the class this year. She said, "I'd like to see the class go on a field trip to a place were we have never gone before. Their is a new history museum nearby, and I here that its very interesting. I'm really glad your printing this interview. It will help more students learn about my idea. Our class has it's work cut out for it if where going to get everything done that we'd like to do this year."

Lola asks that you tell her about you're ideas for the class this year. She is very happy and proud to serve as class president.

A. *Now, correctly rewrite the article.*

_____

_____

_____

_____

_____

_____

_____

_____

_____

_____

B. *Follow directions to write sentences below.*

1. Write three sentences about your school. Correctly use one of the words below in each sentence.

   were   we're   where

_____

_____

_____

2. Write two sentences about your neighborhood. Correctly use one of the words below in each sentence.

   who's   whose

_____

_____

BOOK REVIEW

Read the book review. The writer has made some mistakes with adjectives used to compare. Use proofreading marks to correct the mistakes.

REMEMBER!

- For most adjectives, add *-er* to compare two people, places, or things.
  The lunchroom is bigger than my classroom.

- For most adjectives, add *-est* to compare more than two people, places, or things.
  The gym is the biggest room in the whole school.

- Use the word *good* to describe one person, place, or thing. Use the word *better* to describe two people places or things. Use the word *best* to describe three or more.
  This is a good drawing.
  This drawing is better than the other one.
  This drawing is the best drawing of all.

- Remember. Use these marks to take away one word and add another.
  This drawing is ~~gooder~~ *better* than the other one.

Little House on the Prairie

by Jonas Meyer

I read two books last month. The one I thought was best was <u>Little House on the Prairie</u>. In fact, I think it might be the better book I have ever read. It is certainly not one of the shorter books I have ever read.

The book told about many adventures Laura had with her family. The scarier part of all the parts in the book was the part that told about the whole family getting sick.

The characters in the book are wise. Some might say Pa is the wiser of all, but I think Laura is. I also think she is the smarter of all the characters.

This book was written by Laura Ingalls Wilder. She is my favoritest author. I think <u>Little House on the Prairie</u> is gooder than the last Wilder book I read.

I recommend this book to everyone. I think you will find it is one of the bestest books you will ever read.

GO!

Now, correctly write the book review.

_____

_____

_____

_____

_____

_____

_____

_____

_____

_____

_____

_____

_____

_____

_____

_____

_____

_____

_____

SUMMER BLOG POST

Read the blog post. The writer has made some mistakes with adverbs and adjectives. Use proofreading marks to correct the mistakes.

REMEMBER!

- Do not confuse adjectives and adverbs.
- Adjectives describe people, places, or things.
  You have a good dog.
- Adverbs can tell how, when, and where action happens.
  Your dog does tricks well.

Summer at the Zoo

Dear Students and Teachers:

I am having a best summer than I had last year. I am visiting my cousin. She works in a zoo. I got to spend part of the day at work with her last week. She does her job really good. I think I want to work in a zoo when I'm older.

Yesterday was the worstest day since I got here. My aunt and I were supposed to work in the petting zoo, but it rained all day. My aunt felt sick. She had a cold. Today is gooder, though. The sun is shining. I asked my aunt how she's feeling, and she said, "I'm good. Thanks."

I'll try to post pictures on the blog next week. I'll also bring plenty of pictures when I come back to school in the fall. Summer always seems like the shorter of all the seasons, so we'll all be back at school before we know it. Hope everyone is having the bestest summer ever.

Sincerely,

Leo Tang

GO!

Now, correctly rewrite the blog post.

_____

_____

_____

_____

_____

_____

_____

_____

_____

_____

_____

_____

_____

_____

_____

_____

CLASSIFIEDS

Read the ad. The writer has made some spelling mistakes. Use proofreading marks to take away the misspelled words and add the correct words.

REMEMBER!

- It is important to spell correctly. Some words are often misspelled. Here are some examples.

  address already because could
  enough neighbor receive said
  tonight trouble world

- Practice will help you remember correct spelling.

Colors of the World

Come to the big sale at Colors of the Wurld Art Store. We have everything you need for your

art projeckts!

We new you'd bin waiting for this sale. We wunt you to hav all the supplys

you need. Hour store is diffrunt frum uther stores. We hav plentie of

peepul to help you. We hav hundreds of thingz on hour shelfs.

Do you like to writ

with a speshul kind

of pin? You will

finde it here!

Do you like to use stikers

with yur frends? We have

evury kind of stiker you can

think uv! We receive new ones

evury weak.

Our adress is 890 Rainbow Lane. You will have no trubel finding us.

We are acros the stret from the skool! Kome sea us soon!

Now, correctly rewrite the ad.

Colors of the World

Oh, Yeah? Proof It! Grade 3

65

COMICS

The Case of the Missing Pumpkin and Mice

by Gina Dovis

I have not never seen such a confusing case.

Whut did you sea?

Their was a pumpkin. They're were mice. Then they disapeared.

Whut hapuned nexst?

I saw a coach. It was the most beutifulest coach I have evur seen.

And aftur that?

A women got owt of the coach. Her name wuz Cinderella.

And aftur that?

They're wuz a big dans. I went insid.

Did you go bak outsid latur?

Yes, the coach wuz gone! I couldn't not tell were it had gone.

Folow the coach's trail. Yull find a punkin and sum mice!

Now, correctly rewrite the comic.

The Case of the Missing Pumpkin and Mice

by Gina Dovis

TIGER NEWS

NEWS

NEWS

Read the article. The writer has made some mistakes with capital letters, abbreviations, end marks, commas, quotation marks, and punctuation of titles. Use proofreading marks to correct the mistakes.

REMEMBER!

- Remember what you have learned about capital letters, abbreviations, and end marks. Remember what you have learned about commas, quotation marks, and underlining. Remember what you have learned about apostrophes and spelling.
- Remember proofreading marks you have learned. Turn to page 5 if you want to review the marks.

Castles

by Rosa Banc

We have been studying the Middle Ages in ms kerr's class. We have just finished reeding a book titled Great castles Of The middle Ages. It is filed with informashun abowt moats castles and knights.

Whut do you thingk it wud have been like to liv in the Middle Ages. Europeans livied in a land of lords ladies and knights. Rich lords lived in castles.

The lord and his familie livied in the center uv the castle In the castle, they're were sleeping rooms a dining hall and a kitchun. There where also rooms with swords bows and other weapons.

Their was a moat arownd the castle? It was filed with watur. This helpt to proteckt the peepul in the castle.

What wud Europeans from the Middle Ages think abowt life today I cant evun imagin!

Oh, Yeah? Proof It! Grade 3

GO!

Now, correctly rewrite the article.

_____

_____

_____

_____

_____

_____

_____

_____

_____

_____

_____

_____

_____

_____

_____

_____

_____

_____

TIGER NEWS
ABOUT OUR STUDENTS

Read the article. The writer has made some mistakes with subject-verb agreement. Use proofreading marks to correct the mistakes.

REMEMBER!

• A verb must agree with its subject.

The boy goes to school.

The boys go to school.

The girl races.

The girls race.

• Remember the marks for adding and taking away words. Turn to page 5 if you need to review the marks.

Music

by Bob Johnston

I has been playing the piano, guitar, and violin for three years. I is happy to share information about these instruments.

The piano are part of the string family of musical instruments. The violin and the guitar are also string instruments. Some strings is plucked. This is true of the guitar. Players rubs strings of some other instruments. This is true of the violin. A player hit keys to make strings on a piano move.

The thickness, length, and tightness of a string works together to make a high or low note. A high note comes from a thin string on a guitar. A high note on a piano come from a shorter string. On a guitar, you makes a string shorter by pressing on it.

I thinks about all my rules and lessons. Then I plays the instruments. My friends and I likes to play in the orchestra at school. We looks forward to playing in a concert soon.

GO!

Now, write about one of your hobbies.

- ☐ Include an article title and your name.
- ☐ Tell why you like the hobby.
- ☐ Tell how you do the hobby.
- ☐ Include at least two paragraphs.
- ☐ Make sure all verbs agree with their subjects.
- ☐ Underline all subjects. Circle all verbs.

_____

_____

_____

_____

_____

_____

_____

_____

_____

_____

_____

_____

_____

_____

_____

_____

LETTERS TO THE EDITOR

Read the letter to the editor. The writer forgot to finish some of the sentences. Do not make any changes to complete sentences. Correct the fragments by adding more information you think of yourself. Be sure the sentences make sense.

REMEMBER!

• A sentence tells a complete thought. It includes a subject and a verb.
  Sentence: My neighbor's cat walks on the fence.

• A fragment does not tell a complete thought. It does not include a subject and a verb.
  Fragment: My neighbor's cat.
  Fragment: Walks on the fence.

• Remember the marks to add and take away.

My neighbor's cat. *walks on the fence*

My neighbor's cat Walks on the fence.

New School Garden

Dear Editor:

I was glad to read the article about the school garden. Everyone in our class would like to see

a new garden at school. We are all offering to help. Here are our ideas.

1. Many flowers of different colors.

2. Students from all grades.

3. The larger seeds.

4. Some small plants.

5. Dig spots for seeds.

6. Take turns watering.

7. Will work hard.

Thank your for printing my letter. Really excited about the garden.

Sincerely,

Mena Lakshmi

Mena Lakshmi

GO!

Now, correctly rewrite the letter to the editor. Include the information you have added.

_____

_____

_____

_____

_____

_____

_____

_____

_____

_____

_____

_____

_____

_____

_____

_____

_____

_____

TIGER NEWS

STUDENT STORIES AND IDEAS

Read the article. The writer has written the whole article as one long paragraph. Use proofreading marks to show where each new paragraph should start.

REMEMBER!

- Every sentence in a paragraph should tell about the topic, or main idea, of the paragraph. New paragraphs are important in making writing clear.
- Use this mark to show a new paragraph. ⁋

   Field day was fun. Many people came to watch and play the games. The crowd was the biggest we

have ever had. The day was really hot, so we served plenty of water. We also served juice and sandwiches.

People got very hungry and thirsty. There were ten events. One of the favorite events was the sack race. Everyone wanted to be part of that one.

Seasons

by Maria Sol

It is hard to think of a favorite season. There are things I like about each one. Each season offers so much. Winter snow is something I always enjoy. I like to sit inside and stay warm by the fire. Throwing snowballs is so much fun! Spring is wonderful, too. Flowers bloom, and leaves grow back on trees. Everything seems new during spring. Summer is fantastic! We can swim. We can go on vacation. Days are usually warm and sunny during summer. Fall is special in a way that is all its own. Leaves turn many colors. They swirl gently to the ground. There is just a little cool nip in the air. What a wonderful season!

A. *Correctly rewrite the article.*

_____

_____

_____

_____

_____

_____

_____

_____

_____

_____

_____

_____

_____

_____

B. *Explain how you decided to start the new paragraphs.*

_____

_____

_____

TIGER NEWS
STUDENT STORIES AND IDEAS

Read the article. The writer has made some mistakes. Use proofreading marks to correct the writer's mistakes.

REMEMBER!

- Remember what you have learned about capital letters, abbreviations, and end marks. Remember what you have learned about commas, quotation marks, and underlining. Remember what you have learned about apostrophes and spelling. Remember what you have learned about subject-verb agreement, complete sentences, and paragraphs.

- Remember proofreading marks you have learned. Turn to page 5 if you need to review the marks.

Across the Ice

by Oscar Insky

I wud like to skate in the Olympics won day. Fur now, I praktice hard. Its tough to get up early in the morning. But i do it almost evury day uv the weak. I can sea results wen i work hard. my coach say he kan tell a big diffurunce? I askt my coach, Do you thingk i kan go too the Olympics wun day?" he sed he thought it cud be possibul. I wuz excited. Yesterday my frend sed she wud like to wach me skate. I sed "I have a competition soon. You kan come with my familie. Next weak, i will praktis for an xtra day? I will be getting redy to lurn a knew trick. i wil skate my bestest. Whut a gud time Ill have they're?

GO!

Now, correctly rewrite the article.

_____

_____

_____

_____

_____

_____

_____

_____

_____

_____

_____

_____

_____

_____

_____

_____

_____

_____

NEWS

Read the article. The writer has made some mistakes. Use proofreading marks to correct the writer's mistakes.

Groundhog Day

by Ms. Fatima Sten

Groundhog Day hapens evury year on february 2. Their is an old storie about Groundhog Day. it says groundhogs come out of they're burrows on this day? Does the groundhog see it's shadoe. If it does, spring is supozed too be six Weeks away. what hapens if it doesnt see it's shadoe? Well spring is supozed too be early.

Is the story true. scientists no that clear skys in february ofen come with cold whether. And clowdy Febuary days are ofen warmer. We really cud figure that out without a groundhog.

Reporters go to a speshul toun in pennsylvania on Groundhog Day. They weight for a groundhog named phil to come out of it's burrow. The reporters don't never know whut two expect. last year, one reporter said, I think its fun to weight for the groundhog two come owt of it's burrow."

does the groundhog named phil really let us no about whether spring is coming? Well hes been right only about half of the time. But its still fun to watch for him evury year.

GO!

Now, correctly rewrite the article.

_____

_____

_____

_____

_____

_____

_____

_____

_____

_____

_____

_____

_____

_____

_____

_____

_____

_____

_____

Read the information and the letter. The writers have made some mistakes. Use proofreading marks to correct the writers' mistakes.

New Helmet

This are a letter from Mandy Smith. she bot a new helmet with money she had saved. She ordered it online? The helmet arrived. The strap on the helmet were broked. Called to ask for a new helmet. A recorded voice said "Pleeze leeve yur message after The tone.

Mandy left a message. Noone never called her back. She rote this letter to the Company. the Company sent her a knew helmet. mandy wanted to share her letter to show others how too let a Company know about problums.

Mandy recieved a knew helmut! you can try this kind of letter, two? It cud help you.

Dear mr Vlank:

I bot a helmut from yur Company. I recieved it last tuesday. i couldnt beleive it, but the helmut were broked. I also ordered gloves wrist guards and elbow guards. they was fine

I cant skate with my frends. the strap on my helmut are broken Pleeze help. I payed alot of money. I wud like to order frum yur Company again. It have always been an excullent Company. it have been the better of all helmut companys online. Pleeze send a new helmut? Thank you

Sincerely

Mandy Smith

Mandy smith

GO!

Now, correctly rewrite the information and the letter.

_____

_____

_____

_____

_____

_____

_____

_____

_____

_____

_____

_____

_____

_____

_____

_____

_____

TIGER NEWS

NEWS

Read the ad. The writer has made some mistakes. Use proofreading marks to correct the writer's mistakes.

REMEMBER!

Turn to page 5 if you need to review the marks.

a Nite with the Drama Club

The clinton elementary school will hav a nite with the actors on thurs, apr 30. They're will bee short scenes with singing dancing and acting All of the actors has bin praktising very hard. This is the longer they have praktised for all of there shows.

mr hanks have been wurking with the students. The student's familys have also bin helping.

Wud you like too bee part of this wunderful nite. Just buy yur tikets soon. Be a fun nite for the hole familie.

These are the poems and songs the actors will perform.

• stopping by woods On A Snowy Evening

• singing My Heart Out For you

• working On The Railroad"

• "cant stop The Rain

Actors has written a scene based on they're favurite book. The book's title are "a sign Of The Times today.

Now, correctly rewrite the ad.

Four Corners
by Rick Sanchez

Have you made any ... capital letters. Use marks to correct the mistakes.

- A proper noun begins with a capital letter and names a specific person, place, or thing.
  Proper Nouns: Rover, Chicago, Doctor Gomez
- Common nouns: dog, city, doctor
- This is how you show a change from a capital letter to a lowercase letter.
  She and I went to the store.
- The word *I* is always capitalized.
- This is how you show a change from a lowercase letter to a capital letter.

Doctor

chicago

Anika Ross has stood in four States at the same time! Anika is one of the new Students in third Grade this year. She is in Mr. Gold's class.

Anika moved to our Town from new mexico. Anika has shared many interesting Stories about her life in new mexico. there are excellent hiking trails near her old home. her family often went on Hikes.

Anika enjoys Soccer. She was the star Goalie on her old team. Anika is looking forward to the tryouts for our School's team.

what was Anika's most interesting story of all? She has stood in four States at one time. Really! Did you know that i can do this? others can do this, too. How? they can visit the four corners monument.

where is the four corners monument? how can People stand in four States at once there? Take a look at a map, you will see that arizona, colorado, utah, and new mexico all share a boundary. This boundary is at the four corners monument. When you stand at the monument, this is the Place where all four States meet. we welcome anika to our School. we all look forward to getting to know her better.

page 6

- Make sure to begin all sentences with a capital letter.
- Make sure to begin all common nouns with a lowercase letter.
- Make sure to begin all proper nouns with a capital letter.

Students' article should include correct capitalization, as well as article title, details of an event in the student's town, names of people, and the name of the town.

page 7

☐☐☐

Interview with Hassan Janara
by Claire Grand

... letters. Use proofreading marks to correct the mistakes.

This week, I interviewed Hassan Janara about his Cousin's Company. hassan's cousin takes People on Tours at the statue of liberty when they visit new york city. visitors must ride on a Boat to get to the Statue.

Hassan told me about his visit to the statue of liberty. His Cousin explained that the statue was planned and built in france. It was planned by a Sculptor named frederic auguste bartholdi.

The Statue was too big to ship to the united States. workers had to take it apart! Then, they packed the 350 pieces and put them on a ship.

Hassan's Cousin told Visitors that the torch held in the statue's right Hand burned for a very long time. But the torch started to wear out, and it was damaged by Water. It was replaced by an electric torch.

Hassan can't wait to visit his Cousin in new york city again. On his next Trip, Me hopes to go to Art Museums and tour a Television Station.

page 8

Interview with Hassan Janara
by Claire Grand

This week, I interviewed Hassan Janara about his cousin's company. Hassan's cousin takes people on tours at the statue of liberty when they visit new york city. Visitors must ride on a boat to get to the Statue.

Hassan told me about his visit to the statue of liberty. His cousin explained that the statue was planned and built in france. It was planned by a Sculptor named frederic auguste bartholdi.

The Statue was too big to ship to the united states. workers had to take it apart! Then, they packed the 350 pieces and put them on a ship.

People in the united states had to raise Money to pay for a base for the Statue. It took a great deal of work to put the Statue together and place it on the base.

hassan's cousin told Visitors that the torch held in the statue's right Hand burned for a very long time. But the torch started to wear out, and it was damaged by Water. It was replaced by an electric torch.

Hassan can't wait to visit his Cousin in new york city again. On his next Trip, Me hopes to go to Art Museums and tour a Television Station.

page 9

Note the changes you made to the article. Then, rewrite the article correctly.

Interview with Hassan Janara

by Claire Grand

This week, I interviewed Hassan Janara about his cousin's company. Hassan's cousin takes people on tours at the Statue of Liberty when they visit New York City. Visitors must ride on a boat to get to the statue.

Hassan told me about his visit to the Statue of Liberty. His cousin explained that the statue was planned and built in France. It was planned by a sculptor named Frederic Auguste Bartholdi.

The statue was too big to ship to the United States. Workers had to take it apart! Then, they packed the 350 pieces and put them on a ship.

People in the United States had to raise money to pay for a base for the statue. It took a great deal of work to put the statue together and place it on the base.

Hassan's cousin told visitors that the torch held in the statue's right hand burned for a very long time. But the torch started to wear out, and it was damaged by water. It was replaced by an electric torch.

Hassan can't wait to visit his cousin in New York City again. On his next trip, he hopes to go to art museums and tour a television station.

Bike World Sale

Come to Bike World! We have the finest bikes in miami.

The first five People who come on monday, march 5, will receive free bike Horns.

bike world
691 ling street
miami, Florida

we have the best prices in our City!

The sale will last all Week.
The sale will start on monday, march 5.
The sale will end on sunday, march 11.
do not miss this great sale!

Ask shop owner maria sanchez about special prices for Students from zane elementary school.

☆ don't forget to check back for our big sale on july 4, independence day. ☆

page 10

Bike World Sale

Come to Bike World! We have the finest bikes in Miami.

The first five people who come on Monday, March 5, will receive free bike horns.

Bike World
691 Ling Street
Miami, Florida

We have the best prices in our city!

The sale will last all week.
The sale will start on Monday, March 5.
The sale will end on Sunday, March 11.
Do not miss this great sale!

Ask shop owner Maria Sanchez about special prices for students from Zane Elementary School.

☆ Don't forget to check back for our big sale on July 4, Independence Day. ☆

page 11

page 12

Sarah, plain And Tall
by Miyoko Chong

I was excited about writing this book review. The book was excellent. The characters made me think about the song adventures with the title "we are on the trail." Why? The characters live on the prairie. They give the reader a feeling of being on a trail and going in a direction to find home.

The main characters at the beginning of the book are a father and his children. Caleb and Anna. The father writes to Sarah. She is in Maine. She comes to visit the family. Everyone gets along well.

Still, Sarah misses her old home far away. The father and his children don't want Sarah to leave. Does she stay, or does she go? Guess you'll have to read the book to discover the answer.

I was inspired by this book written by Patricia MacLachlan. I was inspired that I wrote a poem about living on the prairie. The title of the poem is "Living To Work And working To Live."

Next month, our school drama club will do a play based on the book. The play is called "a new Life For Caleb And Anna." I plan to write a review of the play next month. Watch for it in our newspaper.

word is the first word of the title.

The Wizard of Oz

Cam Jansen and the
Mystery of the Dinosaur Bones

Oh Yeah? Proof It! Grade 3

page 13

A. *Correctly rewrite all of the titles from the article.*

Sarah, Plain and Tall

"We Are on the Trail"

"Living to Work and Working to Live"

"A New Life for Caleb and Anna"

B. *Correctly write titles below. Underline the book title. Place quotation marks around poem, play, and song titles.*

The title of one of my favorite books:

> Answers will vary, but should show correct punctuation and capitalization for a book title, a song title, a poem title, and a play title.

The title of one of my favorite songs:

The title of one of my favorite poems:

The title of one of my favorite plays:

Oh Yeah? Proof It! Grade 3

page 14

...important words a pronoun or of the title word is the first word of the title
- Begin a sentence with a capital letter.
- Begin a proper noun with a capital letter. Days of the week, months of the year, and holidays begin with a capital letter.
- The word I is always capitalized.

Lunchroom Changes

september 15, 2011

Dear Ms. tran:

We've seen big changes in the Lunchroom at king elementary school during the past few Years. there is one more change many of us would like to see. We would like to have healthy pizza choices. Last Week, I read "How To make A Healthy pizza." This magazine article had many good Ideas. It was written by someone who lives in California. in california, there have already been many healthy Changes in lunchroom Menus.

I have asked ten Students in each grade for ideas about menu items. everyone has offered pizza as a suggestion. We know the Cooks can use low-fat cheese and whole-wheat crust. We would also like to see Vegetables added as toppings.

maybe we could start the changes in october. If it's hard for the cooks to prepare the pizza, maybe we could just have pizza twice a Week. Maybe we could have Pizza on tuesdays and fridays. Thank you for your time. And thank you for thinking about making this Change.

Sincerely,

Rico Jones

rico jones

14

page 15

Lunchroom Changes

September 15, 2011

Dear Ms. Tran:

We've seen big changes in the lunchroom at King Elementary School during the past few years. There is one more change many of us would like to see. We would like to have healthy pizza choices. Last week, I read "How to Make a Healthy Pizza." This magazine article had many good ideas. It was written by someone who lives in California. In California, there have already been many healthy changes in lunchroom menus.

I have asked ten students in each grade for ideas about menu items. Everyone has offered pizza as a suggestion. We know the cooks can use low-fat cheese and whole-wheat crust. We would also like to see vegetables added as toppings.

Maybe we could start the changes in October. If it's hard for the cooks to prepare the pizza, maybe we could just have pizza twice a week. Maybe we could have pizza on Tuesdays and Fridays. Thank you for your time. And thank you for thinking about making this change.

Sincerely,

Rico Jones

page 16

Let's Sell Wrapping Paper!

it's that time of the Year again! we will be selling wrapping paper to make money for carver elementary school. All the Teachers will have forms to give to their Students.

We hope to have huge sales for our School.

The sale will begin wednesday, october 10. It will continue until the Week after thanksgiving. Tell all your Friends and Neighbors. show them the samples.

Your teacher will tell you about parts of the book titled how To sell wrapping paper. this will give you good Ideas for selling.

16

page 17

Let's Sell Wrapping Paper!

It's that time of the year again! We will be selling wrapping paper to make money for Carver Elementary School. All the teachers will have forms to give to their students.

We hope to have huge sales for our school.

The sale will begin Wednesday, October 10. It will continue until the week after Thanksgiving. Tell all your friends and neighbors. Show them the samples.

Your teacher will tell you about parts of the book titled How to Sell Wrapping Paper. This will give you good ideas for selling.

Oh Yeah? Proof It! Grade 3

Answer Key

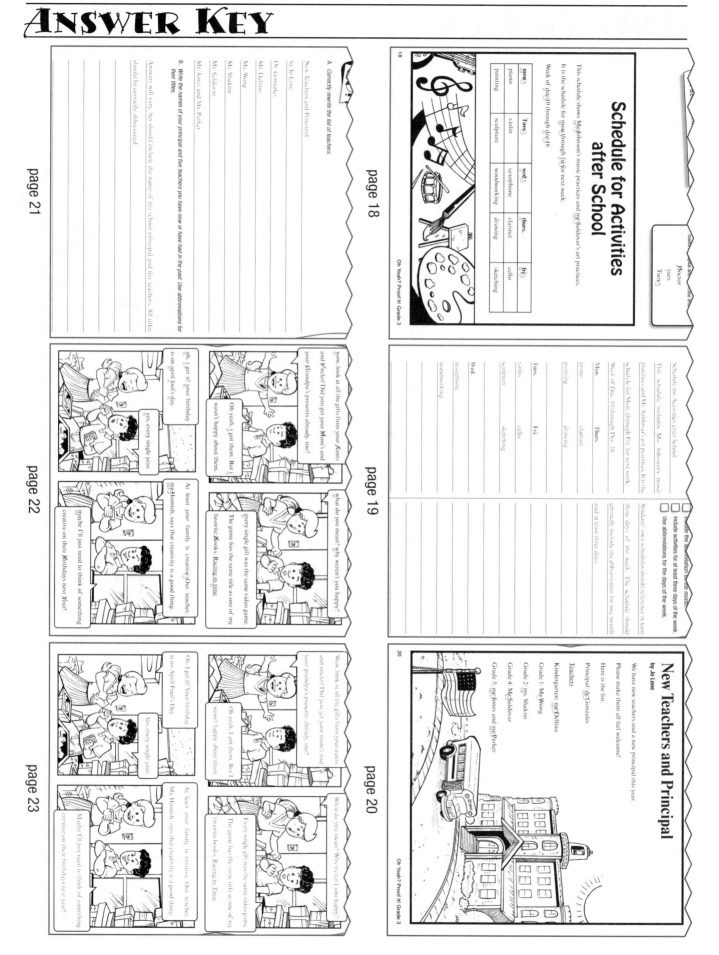

page 24

School Play

Dear Editor:

I read the letter to the editor last week. The letter said we should not have the school play this year. It said we should spend the money on sports instead. Why should we have to give up the school play? What a shame to lose this event?

Many of us would be happy to have a bake sale to raise more money for the play. What else could we do? We could have a car wash or do another activity. How sad it would be to lose the play.

We hope we will be able to vote on this. The students who are actors are willing to work hard to keep our school play.

Sincerely,

Tammy Cruz

Tammy Cruz

- An exclamation ends with an exclamation mark.
- A command usually ends with a period. Please close the door.
- Use this mark to take out an end mark.
- Use this mark to add an end mark.
- This is how to replace one end mark with a different end mark.

What a dog!
This is my dog?
Is this my dog?
What a dog?
Is this my dog?

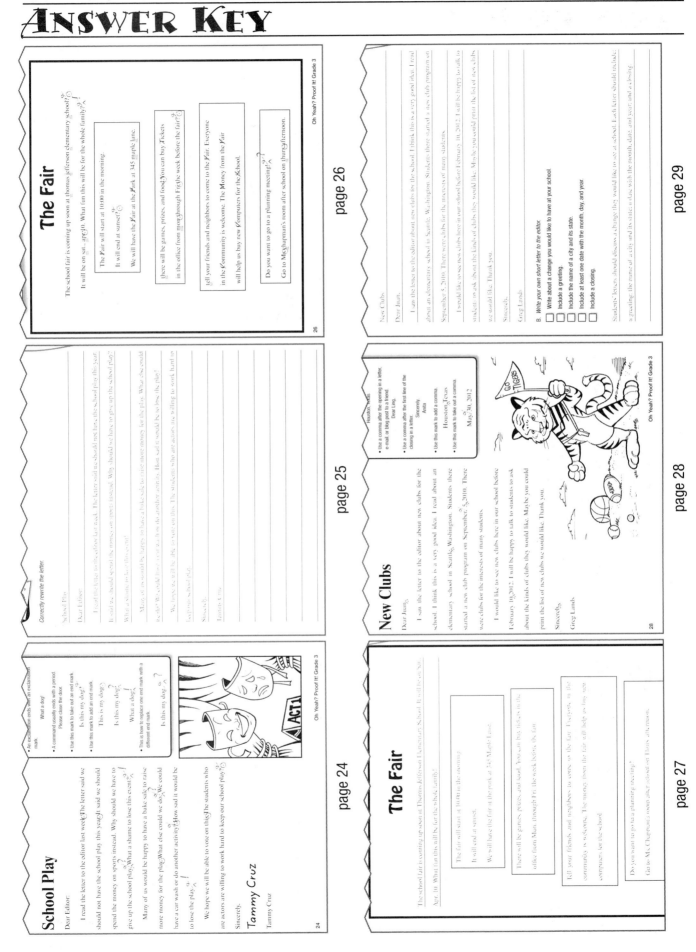

Oh Yeah? Proof It! Grade 3

page 25

Correctly rewrite the letter.

School Play

Dear Editor:

page 26

The Fair

The school fair is coming up soon at thomas jefferson elementary school. What fun this will be for the whole family.

It will be on Sat., apr. 10. What fun this will be for the whole family.

The fair will start at 10:00 in the morning.
It will end at sunset.
We will have the Fair at the Park at 345 maple lane.

there will be games, prizes, and food. You can buy Tickets in the office from mon. through Fri. the week before the fair. Tell your friends and neighbors to come to the Fair. Everyone in the Community is welcome. The Money from the Fair will help us buy new Computers for the School.

Do you want to go to a planning meeting?
Go to Mr. Chapman's room after school on thursd. afternoon.

Oh Yeah? Proof It! Grade 3

page 27

The Fair

The school fair is coming up soon at Thomas Jefferson Elementary School. It will be on Sat., Apr. 10. What fun this will be for the whole family!

The fair will start at 10:00 in the morning.
It will end at sunset.
We will have the fair at the Park at 345 Maple Lane.

There will be games, prizes, and food. You can buy tickets in the office from Mon. through Fri. the week before the fair. Tell your friends and neighbors to come to the fair. Everyone in the community is welcome. The money from the fair will help us buy new computers for the school.

Do you want to go to a planning meeting?
Go to Mr. Chapman's room after school on Thurs. afternoon.

page 28

New Clubs

Dear Juan,

I saw the letter to the editor about new clubs for the school. I think this is a very good idea. I read about an elementary school in Seattle, Washington. Students there started a new club program on September 5, 2010. There were clubs for the interests of many students.

I would like to see new clubs here in our school before February 10, 2012. I will be happy to talk to students to ask about the kinds of clubs they would like. Maybe you could print the list of new clubs we would like. Thank you.

Sincerely,
Greg Lands

- Use a comma after the opening in a letter, e-mail, or blog post to a friend. Dear Ling,
- Use a comma after the first line of the closing in a letter. Sincerely, Anita
- Use this mark to add a comma. Houston, Texas
- Use this mark to take out a comma. May 30, 2012

Houston, Texas

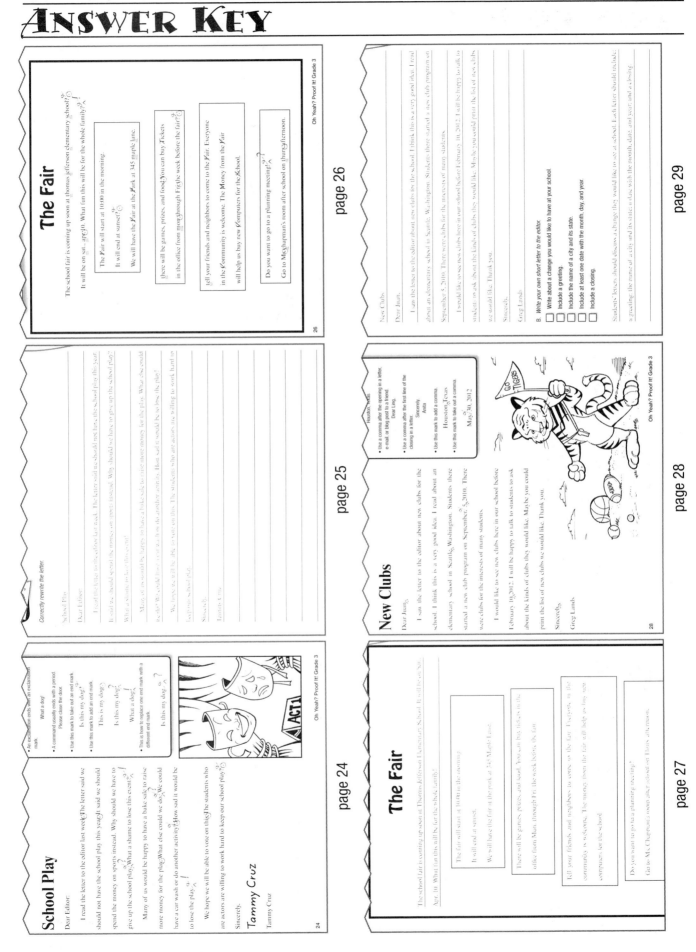

Oh Yeah? Proof It! Grade 3

page 29

New Clubs

Dear Juan,

I saw the letter to the editor about new clubs for the school. I think this is a very good idea. I read about an elementary school in Seattle, Washington. Students there started a new club program on September 5, 2010. There were clubs for the interests of many students.

I would like to see new clubs here in our school before February 10, 2012. I will be happy to talk to students to ask about the kinds of clubs they would like. Maybe you could print the list of new clubs we would like. Thank you.

Sincerely,
Greg Lands

Students' letters should discuss a change they would like to see at school. Each letter should include a greeting, the name of a city and its state, a date with the month, day, and year, and a closing.

B. *Write your own short letter to the editor.*

☐ Write about a change you would like to have at your school.
☐ Include a greeting.
☐ Include the name of a city and its state.
☐ Include at least one date with the month, day, and year.
☐ Include a closing.

ANSWER KEY

The writer has made mistakes with commas. Use proofreading marks to correct the mistakes.

Burritos
by Jan Smart

Yesterday, I spent the day with my grandpa. We made burritos for lunch. Would you like to make burritos? This is how to make them.

You will need beans, cheese, and lettuce. You will also need soft tacos.

First, put a soft taco on a plate. Next, add the beans cheese and lettuce. Finally, roll up the soft taco. Well, that's all you have to do to make this tasty treat!

Do you have a recipe or idea for a tasty treat? Send it to the newspaper. Share it with the school. The newspaper prints recipes from teachers, students, and their friends. We look forward to hearing from you!

page 30

30

- Use commas to separate words in a series. A series is a list of three or more words. We bought eggs, cheese, and bread.
- Remember what you learned about marks for commas.
- Use this mark to add a comma.
- Use this mark to take out a comma.

May, 30, 2012

Houston, Texas

Oh, Yeah? Proof It! Grade 3

☐ Tell the steps to make the food.

Answers will vary, but should show knowledge of correct punctuation with commas. The recipe should name the food in the title and include at least one series. The recipe should tell the steps to make the food and should include at least one of the following words: first, next, finally.

page 31

31

Oh, Yeah? Proof It! Grade 3

"On the Farm"
by Julia Pober

I am happy to review the school play. "On the Farm" was an excellent show. The actors included students from grades two, three, and four. Well, I must say they all did a fine job.

There were a few problems with the show. First, the curtain wouldn't open. Next, part of the curtain fell on the stage. But the show did go on!

The beginning of the play showed farmers, neighbors, and friends working together. There had been very little rain. Yes, the farmers were sad and worried. Everyone was trying to keep the crops alive.

Next, the middle of the play showed that some of the crops were dying. Finally, farmers had a big meeting with the community. Everyone talked, thought, and planned.

page 32

32

- is a list of three or more words. We bought eggs, cheese, and bread.
- Remember what you learned about marks for commas.
- Use this mark to add a comma.
- Use this mark to take out a comma.

May, 30, 2012

Houston, Texas

Did the farmers succeed? No, I'm not going to tell you the answer. You should go see the play for yourself to find out. Support our drama club. Go see the play next weekend!

Oh, Yeah? Proof It! Grade 3

"On the Farm"
by Julia Pober

I am happy to review the school play. "On the Farm" was an excellent show. The actors included students from grades two, three, and four. Well, I must say they all did a fine job.

There were a few problems with the show. First, the curtain wouldn't open. Next, part of the curtain fell on the stage. But the show did go on!

The beginning of the play showed farmers, neighbors, and friends working together. There had been very little rain. Yes, the farmers were sad and worried. Everyone was trying to keep the crops alive.

Next, the middle of the play showed that some of the crops were dying. Finally, farmers had a big meeting with the community. Everyone talked, thought, and planned.

Did the farmers succeed? No, I'm not going to tell you the answer. You should go see the play for yourself to find out. Support our drama club. Go see the play next weekend!

page 33

The writer has made mistakes with commas. Use proofreading marks to correct the mistakes.

"Watching the Sailboats"
by Nav Facs

Ellie and Jamil went to the lake with their dad. The water sparkled. Birds flew. Sailboats dotted the water. Jamil said, "This is the most beautiful day ever!"

Their dad said, "Lunchtime!" Ellie and Jamil dashed to the picnic table.

Dad asked, "Ellie, what would you like on your hot dog?"

Ellie said, "Dad, you know I like my hot dog plain."

Dad asked Jamil what he wanted on his hot dog.

Jamil answered, "Dad, don't be silly. I like everything on my hot dog!"

After lunch, Ellie and Jamil played in the lake. Then they heard a rumble of thunder.

Dad shouted, "It's time to get out of the water."

The three raced to the car. Ellie said, "Jamil, this might have been the most beautiful day ever. But it didn't last!"

Everyone laughed. Dad said, "Ellie, we'll come back to the lake next month."

page 34

34

- Use a comma after a word in a series at the beginning of a sentence.
  "Al, I have your book."
- Use a comma before the beginning quotation mark in dialogue—words that are spoken.
  She said, "Here is your present."
  I asked, "What is it?"
- Use this mark to add a comma.

Houston, Texas

Oh, Yeah? Proof It! Grade 3

"Watching the Sailboats"
by Nav Facs

Ellie and Jamil went to the lake with their dad. The water sparkled. Birds flew. Sailboats dotted the water. Jamil said, "This is the most beautiful day ever!"

Their dad said, "Lunchtime!" Ellie and Jamil dashed to the picnic table.

Dad asked, "Ellie, what would you like on your hot dog?"

Ellie said, "Dad, you know I like my hot dog plain."

Dad asked Jamil what he wanted on his hot dog.

Jamil answered, "Dad, don't be silly. I like everything on my hot dog!"

After lunch, Ellie and Jamil played in the lake. Then they heard a rumble of thunder.

Dad shouted, "It's time to get out of the water."

The three raced to the car. Ellie said, "Jamil, this might have been the most beautiful day ever. But it didn't last!"

Everyone laughed. Dad said, "Ellie, we'll come back to the lake next month."

page 35

ANSWER KEY

page 36

Lost Dog!

is a list of three or more words.
We bought eggs, cheese, and bread.

- Use a comma after a person's name at the beginning of a sentence.
"Al, I have your book."

- Use a comma before the beginning quotation mark in dialogue. Dialogue is words on the page that are spoken.
She said, "Here is your present."
I asked, "What is it?"

- Use this mark to add a comma.

Esperanza has lost her dog. She has written this newspaper blog post to ask everyone to help her find it. She says, "Friends, please help me find my dog. He means so much to my family." Esperanza has written this post to tell more about her lost dog.

Dear Students and Teachers:

Please help me find my dog. He run away yesterday. His name is Coco. He is still a puppy. He was born on May 19, 2011. Coco is brown, black, and red. My neighbors have seen Coco near the park, the library, and our house near school. But she could not catch him. Please call me right away if you see him. Please call to add a comma. We are all trying very hard to find him. Please call me right away if you see him. Thank you!

Sincerely,
Esperanza Juarez

Houston, Texas

page 37

Now, correctly rewrite blog.

Lost Dog!

Esperanza has lost her dog. She has written this newspaper blog post to ask everyone to help her find it. She says, "Friends, please help me find my dog. He means so much to my family." Esperanza has written this post to tell more about her lost dog.

Dear Students and Teachers:

Please help me find my dog. He ran away yesterday. His name is Coco. He is still a puppy. He was born on May 19, 2011. Coco is brown, black, and red. Yesterday, Ms. Shankar saw Coco near school. But she could not catch him. My neighbors have seen Coco near the park, the library, and our house. We are all trying very hard to find him. Please call me right away if you see him. Thank you!

Sincerely,
Esperanza Juarez

page 38

Tasty Delights

Dear Mr. Ruma:

I was interested to read the tuesday interview with Dena Leighton. And i was surprised that her company produces ice cream, milk, and cheese. In the interview, she said, "My family has been in this Business for 100 years."

It was also interesting that her family started the Company the day after thanksgiving. That time of Year is often a time for People to relax. But Ms. Leighton's family was working hard. What a family?

I would like to read Ms. Leighton's book. The article said the title is my life. An ice cream factory. That is the perfect name for the Book. I hope the book tells about the time her Aunt said, "Dena, ice cream is now your life."

Thank You for printing the interview. I enjoyed reading it.

Sincerely,
Olga Pimmer
Olga Pimmer

page 39

Tasty Delights

Dear Mr Ruma:

I was interested to read the Tuesday interview with Dena Leighton. And I was surprised that her company produces ice cream, milk, and cheese. In the interview she said, "My family has been in this business for 100 years."

It was also interesting that her family started the company the day after Thanksgiving. That time of year is often a time for people to relax, but Ms. Leighton's family was working hard. What a family!

I would like to read Ms. Leighton's book. The article said the title is My Life in an Ice Cream Factory. That is the perfect name for the book. I hope the book tells about the time her aunt said, "Dena, ice cream is now your life."

Thank you for printing the interview. I enjoyed reading it.

Sincerely,
Olga Pimmer

page 40

Remember the comma rule. Use proofreading marks to correct the mistakes.

goes inside the quotation marks.
Don said, "Let's go home."
Chitra asked, "What time is it?"

- Use this mark to add a quotation mark.
Don said, "Let's go home."

Successful School Bake Sale
by Hua Chong

The bake sale was a huge success. Mr. Delfy said, "We made $3,000.00 for the school." He explained that students from all grades had worked hard to plan the sale.

Aisha Moore is in third grade. She said, "I was glad to have a chance to help plan such an important event."

Aisha's entire family pitched in to bake and sell. Her dad asked, "When will we start planning for next year?"

Mr. Delfy answered, "We'll start planning in the fall next year. We would really appreciate your help again."

Glen Davis is in fourth grade. He said, "Glen will definitely be a part of the bake sale again next year." Glen was in charge of cookies.

Ms. Win took a break from coaching to take charge of one of the tables at the bake sale. She exclaimed, "This is like having a new kind of teamwork!"

Students and their families will be invited to help next year, too.

page 41

Students' articles/stories will vary but should tell about a real or imaginary event at school or in the community. Each piece should include properly punctuated quotes or dialogue from at least three people.

Answer Key

page 42

Between the Pages

Between the Pages is the best bookstore in town!

We have everything you're looking for. See our specials below.

We have all of these plays!
- Traveling on the Road
- Syn and Rand
- The Great Review

Books on Sale
- Henry and the Paper Route
- The Best School Year Ever
- Charlotte's Web

Sheet Music is on sale for these songs. We have songs for all ages.
- Twinkle, Twinkle, Little Star
- All You Need Is Love
- The Wheels on the Bus

We have books filled with short stories like these:
- Aladdin and the Wonderful Lamp
- Three Words of Wisdom
- Grand Adventures

Oh Yeah? Proof It! Grade 3

- Remember the proofreading mark to add a quotation mark.
- Use this mark to add underlining.

Don't say, "Let's go home."

Ramona Quimby, Age 8

page 43

Responses will vary, but each should be correctly punctuated. Students should not include any of the titles from the ad on page 42.

Book

Play

Song

Short Story

Oh Yeah? Proof It! Grade 3

page 44

Greetings from Earth
by Nita Hamlin

This week's story is science fiction. It is written in the form of a letter to creatures on another Planet. The letter is from a visitor to Earth.

Dear Grilto,

I am writing to tell you about something very strange. I was visiting another Planet. First, I saw creatures carrying heavy things with pages. One human said, "I'm glad we arrived on monday, july 4." There were cold things happening all around Me.

First, I saw creatures carrying heavy things with pages. One human said, "I'm glad we checked out this book from the library." These words were on the front of the book. How do humans... I heard loud noises. A human asked a friend, "Did you tell Frank I'm to meet us for the fireworks?" I wasn't sure what fireworks were. Finally, I saw bright colors in the sky. The humans seemed very happy. This must be a custom on their Planet.

I will be glad to get back to our Planet. It will be nice for things to be normal again.

Sincerely,
Griblit

Oh Yeah? Proof It! Grade 3

page 45

Greetings from Earth
by Nita Hamlin

This week's story is science fiction. It is written in the form of a letter to creatures on another Planet. The letter is from a visitor to Earth.

Dear Grilto,

I am writing to tell you about something very strange. I was visiting another Planet. I arrived on

Monday, July 4. There were cold things happening all around me.

First, I saw creatures carrying heavy things with pages. One human said, "I'm glad we checked out this book from the library." These words were on the front of the book. How do I celebrate Independence as this book from the library.

Next, I heard loud noises. A human asked a friend, "Did you tell Mr. Frank I'm to meet us for the fireworks?" I wasn't sure what fireworks were. Finally, I saw bright colors in the sky. (or?) The humans seemed very happy. This must be a custom on their planet.

I will be glad to get back to our planet. It will be nice for things to be normal again.

Sincerely,
Griblit

page 46

Dream On!
by Reve Craddock

I think I'm trapped.
I can't get out.
My throat is tight,
but I won't shout.

I see a friend.
I'll look ahead.
Well hope this dream
won't cause more dread.

I'm pounding the door
and kicking the wood.
It doesn't open
as it should.

And then the light
comes into sight.
I'll open up my eyes
Now I'm awake.
It's time to take
a step into the day.

I'll try to yell.
I'll try to scream.
I hadn't planned
on this bad dream.

No Wait!
I'd rather sleep longer instead.

- Use this mark to add an apostrophe.
- Use this mark to take away an apostrophe.

can + not = can't
I + am = I'm
you + would = you'd
don't

Oh Yeah? Proof It! Grade 3

page 47

Dream On!
by Reve Craddock

I think I'm trapped.
I can't get out.
My throat is tight,
but I won't shout.

I see a friend.
I'll look ahead.
We'll hope this dream
won't cause more dread.

I'm pounding the door
and kicking the wood.
It doesn't open
as it should.

And then the light
comes into sight.
I'll open up my eyes
Now I'm awake.
It's time to take
a step into the day.

I'll try to yell.
I'll try to scream.
I hadn't planned
on this bad dream.

No Wait!
I'd rather sleep longer instead.

ANSWER KEY

page 48

homemade out mixed-up mistakes. Use proofreading marks to correct the mistakes.

Our Team Wins!
by Pat Stroger

We have the best basketball team in the city! Our teams players were amazing in the game last week.

Each player's hard work was clear.

Students filled the gym before the game began. Many students' shirts showed the teams name.

Play was tough during the beginning of the game. All the parents' voices were hushed.

Everyone watched.

The coaches' voices were loud as they called out to players. We all watched and listened.

The gym was very quiet before a big play. Then, one boy's drink spilled onto the gym floor.

Everyone had to wait for the floor to be cleaned. Finally, the game started again.

We weren't sure until the end who would win. At the last minute, we won! The players' cheers were very loud. We are now the city champions!

[sidebar box:]
A possessive noun is used to show that someone owns something. For most singular nouns, add an apostrophe and the letter s.

two girls' hats — girl's hat
three friends' skates — friend's skates
four dogs' tails — dog's tail

• For most plural nouns, add an apostrophe after the s.
girls

• Use this mark to add an apostrophe.

48   Oh Yeah? Proof It! Grade 3

page 49

Now, correctly rewrite the sports report.

Our Team Wins!

by Pat Stroger

We have the best basketball team in the city! Our team's players were amazing in the game last week. Each player's hard work was clear.

Students filled the gym before the game began. Many students' shirts showed the team's name.

Play was tough during the beginning of the game. All the parents' voices were hushed. Everyone watched.

The coaches' voices were loud as they called out to players. We all watched and listened. The gym was very quiet before a big play. Then, one boy's drink spilled onto the gym floor. Everyone had to wait for the floor to be cleaned. Finally, the game started again.

We weren't sure until the end who would win. At the last minute, we won! The players' cheers were very loud. We are now the city champions!

page 50

homemade out mixed-up apostrophes. Use proofreading marks to correct the mistakes.

Tornado Hits Our Town
by Shane Ville

A tornado hit our town last week. It hit at night. Most of us were at home asleep. Many of us didn't even hear the tornado or the warning siren. No one in town was hurt.

Our school's front door was blown open. Water, paper, and leaves were blown into the main hall. Workers came to help the next morning. At first, they couldn't even see the floor underneath everything that had blown inside the hall. Then they cleared away the mess.

The teacher's said they'd like to return to school as soon as possible. But one teacher's room was still a mess on Wednesday. Other teachers' rooms did not take too long to clean. School should be open again next week. We'll have to make up the lost days at the beginning of summer vacation.

I'd like to thank the teachers who helped us put together this issue of the newspaper. I can't imagine it would have been possible without them.

50

page 51

Tornado Hits Our Town

by Shane Ville

A tornado hit our town last week. It hit at night. Most of us were at home asleep. Many of us didn't even hear the tornado or the warning siren. No one in town was hurt.

Our school's front door was blown open. Water, paper, and leaves were blown into the main hall. Workers came to help the next morning. At first, they couldn't even see the floor underneath everything that had blown inside the hall. Then they cleared away the mess.

The teachers said they'd like to return to school as soon as possible. But one teacher's room was still a mess on Wednesday. Other teachers' rooms did not take too long to clean. School should be open again next week. We'll have to make up the lost days at the beginning of summer vacation.

I'd like to thank the teachers who helped us put together this issue of the newspaper. I can't imagine it would have been possible without them.

page 52

commas, quotation marks, and apostrophes. Use proofreading marks to correct the mistakes.

Birthday surprises
by Linus Paolo

I checked the Mail.

It was there!

I quickly ripped it open, or "!

I saw a card, note, and a bit of cash.

This was exactly what I'd been hoping.

The Birthday money was what I'd wanted.

I took the card inside.

I called my Aunt.

I said, "I'm so happy that I could almost cry."

My Aunt was happy that I was glad.

She told Me right away.

And then she had another surprise.

She said, "I'm coming to see you next Tuesday."

What a wonderful day.

I couldn't wait to see my Aunt.

We could go together to Mr. Rob's store to spend my cash right on my Birthday!

[sidebar note:] ...marks, and other punctuation. Turn to page 53 and need to review the marks.

52   Oh Yeah? Proof It! Grade 3

page 53

Birthday Surprises

by Linus Paolo

I checked the mail.

It was there!

I quickly ripped it open, for "!

I saw a card, a note, and a bit of cash.

This was exactly what I'd been hoping.

My birthday surprises were nearly complete.

The birthday money was what I'd wanted.

I took the card inside.

I called my aunt.

I said, "I'm so happy that I could almost cry."

My aunt was happy that I was glad.

She told me right away.

And then she had another surprise.

She said, "I'm coming to see you next Tuesday."

What a wonderful day!

I couldn't wait to see my aunt.

We could go together to Ms. Rob's store to spend my cash right on my birthday!

Oh Yeah? Proof It! Grade 3

ANSWER KEY

Planets
by Gita Chitra

Note to the teacher: Alternative answers are noted in parentheses.

This includes negative contractions. Here are some examples.
didn't couldn't wouldn't can't won't
doesn't hadn't shouldn't

- Use this mark to take away a word.

I don't ~~not~~ like it.
Nobody ~~never~~ goes there.

This book ~~isn't not~~ (isn't/is not) the kind of book we usually review. We ~~haven't never~~ (haven't/have never/haven't ever) written this kind of review before now. Last week, the second graders wrote books about the stars and planets. We are reviewing one of the student's books.

This book does a good job of telling about the solar system. There's ~~not nothing~~ (nothing/not anything) more interesting than a good book. And this book is very good.

The book gives information about Pluto. The writer explains that Pluto is ~~not nowhere~~ (nowhere/not anywhere) near Earth. The book says that Pluto is no longer named as a planet. No one ~~never~~ (ever/[or delete word]) thought this would happen.

I think this student might grow up to be a writer. Her book is very interesting.

54 Oh Yeah? Proof It! Grade 3

page 54

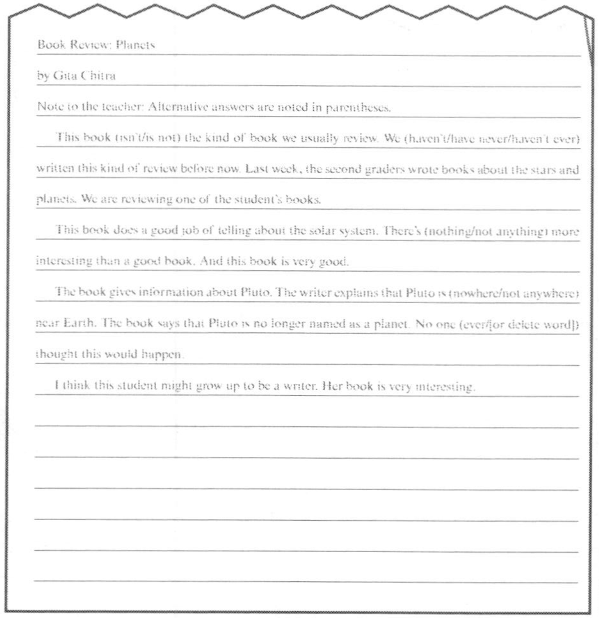

Book Review: Planets

by Gita Chitra

Note to the teacher: Alternative answers are noted in parentheses.

This book (isn't/is not) the kind of book we usually review. We (haven't/have never/haven't ever) written this kind of review before now. Last week, the second graders wrote books about the stars and planets. We are reviewing one of the student's books.

This book does a good job of telling about the solar system. There's (nothing/not anything) more interesting than a good book. And this book is very good.

The book gives information about Pluto. The writer explains that Pluto is (nowhere/not anywhere) near Earth. The book says that Pluto is no longer named as a planet. No one (ever/[or delete word]) thought this would happen.

I think this student might grow up to be a writer. Her book is very interesting.

page 55

Help after the Hurricane

your you're
here hear
its it's
who's whose

- Use these marks to take away one word and add another.

They left ~~there~~ their bats in the gym.

People in Louisiana need everyone's help after the big hurricane. The school is placing this ~~add~~ ad to let you ~~no~~ know how everyone ~~hear~~ here can help. We will be collecting items all ~~weak~~ week.

Please take time to read all the information in this ~~add~~ ad. ~~Were~~ We're all sure you can find a ~~weigh~~ way to help. If you have questions after you have ~~red~~ read the ~~add~~ ad, call the school office.

We will ~~bee~~ be collecting bottled water in the mall parking lot. This is the address. 425 Old River ~~Rode~~ Road

Take tops, slacks, and other ~~close too~~ clothes to the gym at the high school. ~~Its~~ It's at the back of the building.

We will ~~knot~~ not turn away any help you want to offer, ~~sew~~ so please call if you have more ideas.

56 Oh Yeah? Proof It! Grade 3

page 56

Help after the Hurricane

People in Louisiana need everyone's help after the big hurricane. The school is placing this ad to let you know how everyone here can help. We will be collecting items all week.

Please take time to read all the information in this ad. We're all sure you can find a way to help. If you have questions after you have read the ad, call the school office.

We will be collecting bottled water in the mall parking lot. This is the address. 425 Old River Road

Take tops, slacks, and other clothes to the gym at the high school. It's at the back of the building.

We will not turn away any help you want to offer, so please call if you have more ideas.

page 57

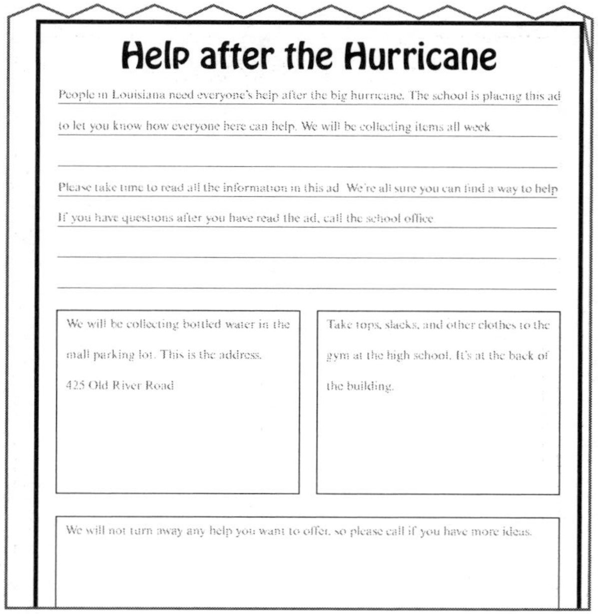

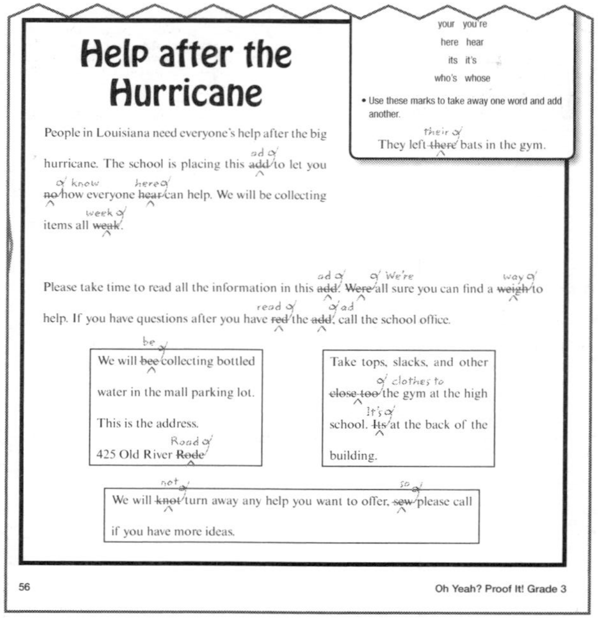

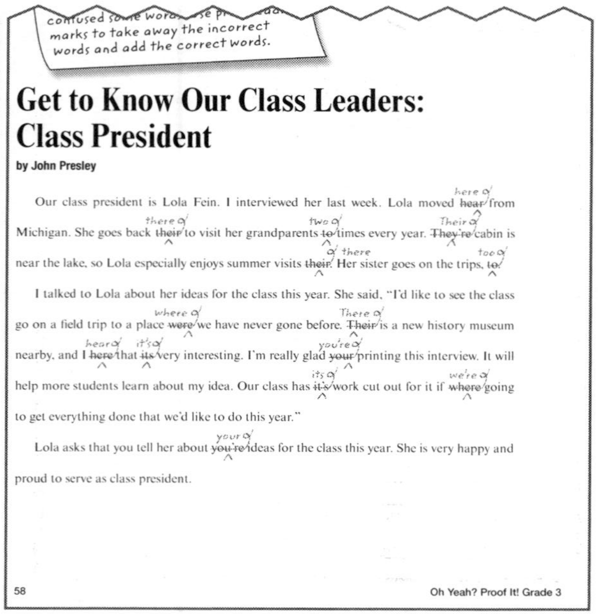

...confused some words. Use proofreading marks to take away the incorrect words and add the correct words.

Get to Know Our Class Leaders: Class President
by John Presley

Our class president is Lola Fein. I interviewed her last week. Lola moved ~~hear~~ here from Michigan. She goes back ~~their~~ there to visit her grandparents ~~to~~ two times every year. ~~They're~~ Their cabin is near the lake, so Lola especially enjoys summer visits ~~their~~ there. Her sister goes on the trips, ~~to~~ too.

I talked to Lola about her ideas for the class this year. She said, "I'd like to see the class go on a field trip to a place ~~were~~ where we have never gone before. ~~Their~~ There is a new history museum nearby, and I ~~here~~ heard that ~~its~~ it's very interesting. I'm really glad ~~your~~ you're printing this interview. It will help more students learn about my idea. Our class has ~~it's~~ its work cut out for it if ~~where~~ we're going to get everything done that we'd like to do this year."

Lola asks that you tell her about ~~you're~~ your ideas for the class this year. She is very happy and proud to serve as class president.

58 Oh Yeah? Proof It! Grade 3

page 58

Get to Know Our Class Leaders: Class President by John Presley

Our class president is Lola Fein. I interviewed her last week. Lola moved here from Michigan. She goes back there to visit her grandparents two times every year. Their cabin is near the lake, so Lola especially enjoys summer visits there. Her sister goes on the trips, too.

I talked to Lola about her ideas for the class this year. She said, "I'd like to see the class go on a field trip to a place where we have never gone before. There is a new history museum nearby, and I hear that it's very interesting. I'm really glad you're printing this interview. It will help more students learn about my idea. Our class has its work cut out for it if we're going to get everything done that we'd like to do this year."

Lola asks that you tell her about your ideas for the class this year. She is very happy and proud to serve as class president.

B. *Follow directions to write sentences below.*

1. Write three sentences about your school. Correctly use one of the words below in each sentence.
   were we're where

   Answers will vary. Each sentence should tell something about the school and correctly include one of these words: *were, we're, where.*

2. Write two sentences about your neighborhood. Correctly use one of the words below in each sentence.
   who's whose

   Answers will vary. Each sentence should correctly include one of these words: *who's, whose.*

page 59

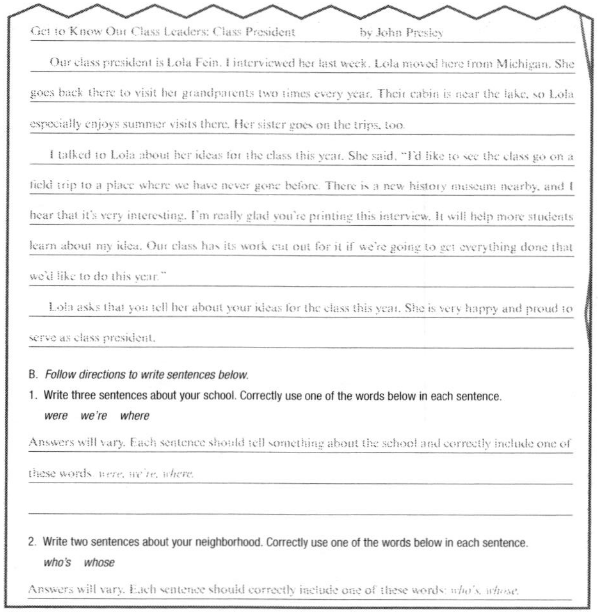

ANSWER KEY

Little House on the Prairie
by Jonas Meyer

- Use the word *good* to describe one person, place, or thing. Use the word *better* to describe two people, places or things. Use the word *best* to describe three or more.
- Remember: Use these marks to take away one word and add another.

I read two books last month. The one I
thought was ~~bad~~ *best* was Little House on the Prairie.

In fact, I think it might be the ~~better~~ *best* book I have
ever read. It is certainly not one of the ~~shorter~~ *shortest*
books I have ever read.

The book told about many adventures Laura
had with her family. The ~~scarier~~ *scariest* part of all the
parts in the book was the part that told about the
whole family getting sick.

The characters in the book are wise. Some
might say Pa is the ~~wiser~~ *wisest* of all, but I think
Laura is. I also think she is the ~~smarter~~ *smartest* of all the
characters.

This book was written by Laura Ingalls Wilder.
She is my ~~favoriter~~ *favorite* author. I think Little House
on the Prairie is ~~gooder~~ *better* than the last Wilder book
I read.

I recommend this book to everyone. I think
you will find it is one of the ~~bestest~~ *best* books you will
ever read.

page 60

Oh Yeah? Proof It! Grade 3   60

Now, correctly write the book review.

Little House on the Prairie

by Jonas Meyer

I read two books last month. The one I thought was best was Little House on the Prairie. In fact,

I think it might be the best book I have ever read. It is certainly not one of the shortest books I have

ever read.

The book told about many adventures Laura had with her family. The scariest part of all the parts

in the book was the part that told about the whole family getting sick.

The characters in the book are wise. Some might say Pa is the wisest of all, but I think Laura is. I

also think she is the smartest of all the characters.

This book was written by Laura Ingalls Wilder. She is my favorite author. And I think Little

House on the Prairie is better than the last Wilder book I read.

I recommend this book to everyone. I think you will find it is one of the best books you will ever

read.

page 61

Oh Yeah? Proof It! Grade 3   61

Summer at the Zoo

Dear Students and Teachers:

I am having a ~~best~~ *better* summer than I had last year. I am visiting my cousin. She works in a

zoo. I got to spend part of the day at work with her last week. She does her job really ~~good~~ *well*.

I think I want to work in a zoo when I'm older.

Yesterday was the ~~worsest~~ *worst* day since I got here. My aunt and I were supposed to work

in the petting zoo, but it rained all day. My aunt felt sick. She had a cold. Today is ~~gooder~~ *better*

though. The sun is shining. I asked my aunt how she's feeling, and she said, "I'm ~~good~~ *well*."

Thanks."

I'll try to post pictures on the blog next week. I'll also bring plenty of pictures when I come

back to school in the fall. Summer always seems like the ~~shorter~~ *shortest* of all the seasons, so we'll all

be back at school before we know it. Hope everyone is having the ~~bestest~~ *best* summer ever.

Sincerely,

Leo Tang

page 62

Oh Yeah? Proof It! Grade 3   62

Summer at the Zoo

Dear Students and Teachers:

I am having a better summer than I had last year. I am visiting my cousin. She works in a zoo. I

got to spend part of the day at work with her last week. She does her job really well. I think I want to

work in a zoo when I'm older

Yesterday was the worst day since I got here. My aunt and I were supposed to work in the petting

zoo, but it rained all day. My aunt felt sick. She had a cold. Today is better, though. The sun is shining.

I asked my aunt how she's feeling, and she said, "I'm well, Thanks."

I'll try to post pictures on the blog next week. I'll also bring plenty of pictures when I come back

to school in the fall. Summer always seems like the shortest of all the seasons, so we'll all be back at

school before we know it. Hope everyone is having the best summer ever

Sincerely,

Leo Tang

page 63

Colors of the World

Come to the big sale at Colors of the World Art Store. We have everything you need for your

art projects!

We knew you'd been waiting for this sale. We want you to have all the supplies you need. Our

store is different from other stores. We have plenty of people to help you. We have hundreds

of things on our shelves.

Do you like to use stickers with your friends? We

have every kind of sticker you can think of? We

receive new ones every week

Do you like to write with a special

kind of pen? You will find it here!

Our address is 890 Rainbow Lane. You will have no trouble finding us. We are across the

street from the school! Come see us soon!

page 65

---

page 64

Oh Yeah? Proof It! Grade 3   64

page 66

by Gina Dovis

Oh Yeah? Proof It! Grade 3

page 67

by Gina Dovis

Oh Yeah? Proof It! Grade 3

Castles

by Rosa Banc

Read the article. The writer has made some mistakes with capital letters, abbreviations, end marks, commas, quotation marks, and punctuation of titles. Use proofreading marks to correct the mistakes.

- Remember what you have learned about capital letters, abbreviations, and end marks. Remember what you have learned about commas, quotation marks, and underlining. Remember what you have learned about apostrophes and spelling.
- Remember proofreading marks you have learned. Turn to page 5 if you want to review the marks.

We have been studying the Middle Ages in Ms. Kerr's class. We have just finished reading a book titled Great Castles Of The middle Ages. It is filled with information about reading and knights. What do you think it would have been like to live in the Middle Ages? Europeans lived in a land of lords, ladies, and knights. Rich lords lived in castles. The lord and his family lived in the center of the castle. There were also sleeping rooms, a dining hall, and a kitchen. There where also rooms with swords, bows, and other weapons. There was a moat around the castle. It was filled with water. This help to protect the people in the castle. What would Europeans from the Middle Ages think about life today? I can't even imagine!

page 68

- Make sure all verbs agree with their subjects. Circle all verbs. Underline all subjects.

Answers will vary. Students should write about a hobby and explain how they participate in the hobby. Include at least two paragraphs, underline all subjects, and circle all verbs. Subject-verb agreement should be correct for all sentences.

Oh Yeah? Proof It! Grade 3

page 69

Castles

by Rosa Banc

We have been studying the Middle Ages in Ms. Kerr's class. We have just finished reading a book titled Great Castles of the Middle Ages. It is filled with information about meats, castles, and knights.

What do you think it would have been like to live in the Middle Ages? Europeans lived in a land of lords, ladies, and knights. Rich lords lived in castles.

The lord and his family lived in the center of the castle. In the castle, there were sleeping rooms, a dining hall, and a kitchen. There were also rooms with swords, bows, and other weapons.

There was a moat around the castle. It was filled with water. This helped to protect the people in the castle.

What would Europeans from the Middle Ages think about life today? I can't even imagine!

page 70

- made some mistakes in this verb agreement. Use proofreading marks to correct the mistakes.

- Remember the marks for adding and taking away words. Turn to page 5 if you need to review the marks.

Music

by Bob Johnston

I have been playing the piano, guitar, and violin for three years. I am happy to share information about these instruments.

The piano are part of the string family of musical instruments. The violin and the guitar are also string instruments. Some strings is plucked. This is true of the guitar. Players make strings of some other instruments. This is true of the violin. A player hit keys to make strings on a piano move.

The thickness, length, and tightness of a string on a guitar work together to make a high or low note. A high note comes from a thin string on a guitar. A high note on a piano comes from a shorter string. On a guitar, you make a string shorter by pressing on it.

I think about all my rules and lessons. Then I play the instruments. My friends and I like to play in the orchestra at school. We look forward to playing in a concert soon.

page 71

Oh Yeah? Proof It! Grade 3

Answer Key

page 72

Remember... yourself. Be sure the sentences make sense.

The ... fence.
Fragment: Walks on the fence.
walks on the fence.
walks on the fence
My neighbor's cat,
Walks on the fence.

- Remember the marks to add and take away.
My neighbor's cat
Walks on the fence.

New School Garden

Dear Editor:

I was glad to read the article about the school garden. Everyone in our class would like to see a new garden at school. We are all offering to help. Here are our ideas.

1. Many flowers of different colors.
2. Students from all grades.
3. The larger seeds.
4. Some small plants.
5. Dig spots for seeds.
6. Take turns watering.
7. Will work hard.

Thank you for printing my letter. Really excited about the garden.

Sincerely,

Mena Lakshmi

Mena Lakshmi

72   Oh Yeah? Proof It! Grade 3

page 73

Now, correctly rewrite the letter to the editor. Include the information you have added.

Answers will vary, as students have been instructed to reveal additional content themselves; however, they should revise fragments to create complete sentences that make sense.

73   Oh Yeah? Proof It! Grade 3

page 74

- Every sentence in a paragraph should tell about the topic, or main idea, of the paragraph. New paragraphs are important in making writing clear.
- Use this mark to show a new paragraph.

Read the article. The writer has written the whole article as one long paragraph. Use proofreading marks to show where each new paragraph should start.

Seasons
by Maria Sol

It is hard to think of a favorite season. There are things I like about each one. Each season offers so much. Winter snow is something I always enjoy. I like to sit inside and stay warm by the fire. Throwing snowballs is so much fun. Spring is wonderful, too. Flowers bloom, and leaves grow back on trees. Everything seems new during spring. Summer is fantastic! We can swim. We can go on vacation. Days are usually warm and sunny during summer. Fall is special in a way that is all its own. Leaves turn many colors. They swirl gently to the ground. There is just a little cool nip in the air. What a wonderful season!

74

page 75

Seasons

by Maria Sol

It is hard to think of a favorite season. There are things I like about each one. Each season offers so much.

Winter snow is something I always enjoy. I like to sit inside and stay warm by the fire. Throwing snowballs is so much fun!

Spring is wonderful, too. Flowers bloom, and leaves grow back on trees. Everything seems new during spring.

Summer is fantastic! We can swim. We can go on vacation. Days are usually warm and sunny during summer.

Fall is special in a way that is all its own. Leaves turn many colors. They swirl gently to the ground. There is just a little cool nip in the air. What a wonderful season!

B. _Explain how you decided to start the new paragraphs._

Answers should indicate that the first paragraph break occurs after the introduction, and each subsequent paragraph break occurs for each new season.

page 76

REMEMBER!
Remember what you have learned about capital letters, abbreviations, and end marks. Remember what you have learned about commas, quotation marks, and underlining. Remember what you have learned about apostrophes and spelling. Remember what you have learned about subject-verb agreement, complete sentences, and paragraphs. Remember proofreading marks you have learned. Turn to page 5 if you need to review the marks.

Read the article. The writer has made some mistakes. Use proofreading marks to correct the writer's mistakes.

Across the Ice
by Oscar Insky

I would like to skate in the Olympics one day. For now, I practice hard. It's tough to get up early in the morning, but I do it almost every day of the week. I can see results when I work hard. My coach says he can tell a big difference. Do you think I can go too? "I asked my coach, "Do you think I can go to the Olympics one day?" He said he thought it could be possible. I was excited. Yesterday, my friend said she would like to watch me skate. I said, "I have a competition soon. You can come with my family." Next week, I will practice for an extra day. I will be getting ready to learn a new trick. I will skate my best. What a good time I'll have there!

76   Oh Yeah? Proof It! Grade 3

page 77

Across the Ice

by Oscar Insky

I would like to skate in the Olympics one day. For now, I practice hard. It's tough to get up early in the morning, but I do it almost every day of the week. I can see results when I work hard. My coach says he can tell a big difference.

I asked my coach, "Do you think I can go to the Olympics one day?" He said he thought it could be possible. I was excited.

Yesterday, my friend said she would like to watch me skate. I said, "I have a competition soon. You can come with my family."

Next week, I will practice for an extra day. I will be getting ready to learn a new trick. I will skate my best. What a good time I'll have there!

Groundhog Day
by Ms. Fatima Sten

Groundhog Day happens every year on February 2. There is an old story about Groundhog Day. It says groundhogs come out of their burrows on that day. Does the groundhog see its shadow? If it does, spring is supposed to be six weeks away, what happens if it doesn't see its shadow? Well, spring is supposed to be early.

Is the story true? Scientists know that clear skies in February often come with cold weather. And cloudy February days are often warmer. We really could figure that out without a groundhog.

Reporters go to a special town in Pennsylvania on Groundhog Day. They wait for a groundhog named Phil to come out of its burrow. The reporters don't ever know what to expect. Last year, one reporter said, "I think it's fun to wait for the groundhog to come out of its burrow."

Does the groundhog named Phil really let us know about whether spring is coming? Well, he's been right only about half of the time. But it's still fun to watch for him every year.

page 78

New Helmet

This is a letter from Mandy Smith. She bought a new helmet with money she had saved. She ordered it online. The helmet arrived. The strap on the helmet was broken. It called to ask for a new helmet. A recorded voice said, "Please leave your message after the tone."

Mandy left a message. No one ever called her back. She wrote this letter to the company. The company sent her a message. Mandy wanted to share her letter to show others how to get a company know about problems.

Mandy received a new helmet. You can try this kind of letter too. It could help you.

Dear Mr. Vlank,

I bought a helmet from your company. I received it last Tuesday. I couldn't believe it, but the helmet was broken. I also ordered gloves, wrist guards, and elbow guards. They were fine.

I can't skate with my friends. The strap on my helmet is broken.

Please help. I would like to order from your company again. It has always been an excellent company. I paid a lot of money. Please send a new helmet. Thank you.

Sincerely,

Mandy Smith

page 81

---

a Nite with the Drama Club

The Clinton Elementary School will have a nite with the actors on Thurs, Apr 30. There will be short scenes with singing, dancing, and acting. All of the actors have been practicing very hard. This is the longest they have practiced for all of their shows.

Mr. Hanks has been working with the students. The students' families have also been helping. Would you like to be part of this wonderful nite? Just buy your tickets soon. It will be a fun nite for the whole family.

These are the poems and songs the actors will perform.

- "Stopping by Woods on a Snowy Evening"
- "Singing My Heart Out For you"
- "Working On the Railroad"
- "Can't stop The Rain"

Actors have written a scene based on their favorite book. The book's title is "A Sign of The Times today."

page 82

New Helmet

This is a letter from Mandy Smith. She bought a new helmet with money she had saved. She ordered it online. The helmet arrived. The strap on the helmet was broken. She called to ask for a new helmet. A recorded voice said, "Please leave your message after the tone."

Mandy left a message. No one ever called her back. She wrote this letter to the Company. The Company sent her a message. Mandy wanted to share her letter to show others how the Company know about problems. Mandy received a new helmet. You can try this kind of letter, too. It could help you.

Dear Mr. Vlank,

I bought a helmet from your Company. I received it last Tuesday. I couldn't believe it, but the helmet was broken. I also ordered gloves, wrist guards, and elbow guards. They were fine.

I can't skate with my friends. The strap on my helmet is broken.

Please help. I would like to order from your Company again. It has always been an excellent Company. I paid a lot of money. Please send a new helmet. Thank you.

Sincerely,

Mandy Smith

page 83

Groundhog Day (cont.)

Groundhog Day happens every year on February 2. There is an old story about Groundhog Day. It says groundhogs come out of their burrows on that day. Does the groundhog see its shadow? If it does, spring is supposed to be six weeks away. What happens if it doesn't see its shadow? Well, spring is supposed to be early.

Is the story true? Scientists know that clear skies in February often come with cold weather. And cloudy February days are often warmer. We really could figure that out without a groundhog.

Reporters go to a special town in Pennsylvania on Groundhog Day. They wait for a groundhog named Phil to come out of its burrow. The reporters don't ever know what to expect. Last year, one reporter said, "I think it's fun to wait for the groundhog to come out of its burrow."

Does the groundhog named Phil really let us know about whether spring is coming? Well, he's been right only about half of the time. But it's still fun to watch for him every year.

page 79

A Night with the Drama Club

The Clinton Elementary School will have a night with the actors on Thurs, Apr 30. There will be short scenes with singing, dancing, and acting. All of the actors have been practicing very hard. This is the longest they have practiced for all of their shows.

Mr. Hanks has been working with the students. The students' families have also been helping. Would you like to be part of this wonderful night? Just buy your tickets soon. It will be a fun night for the whole family.

These are the poems and songs the actors will perform.

- "Stopping by Woods on a Snowy Evening"
- "Singing My Heart Out For You"
- "Working on the Railroad"
- "Can't Stop the Rain"

Actors have written a scene based on their favorite book. The book's title is A Sign of the Times Today.

page 80